Mau Mau: Twenty Years After

Communications 4

AFRIKA-STUDIECENTRUM · LEIDEN

ROBERT BUIJTENHUIJS

Mau Mau: Twenty Years After

The Myth and the Survivors

MOUTON · THE HAGUE · PARIS

Publications in collaboration with the Afrika-Studiecentrum, Leiden:*

Communications

1. M.L. Daneel: The God of the Matopo Hills. An Essay on the Mwari Cult in Rhodesia. 1970
2. M.L. Daneel: Zionism and Faith-Healing in Rhodesia. Aspects of African Independent Churches. 1970
3. P.M. van Hekken & H.U.E. Thoden van Velzen: Land Scarcity and Rural Inequality in Tanzania. Some Case Studies from Rungwe District. 1972

Change and Continuity in Africa

1. Robert Buijtenhuijs: Le Mouvement «Mau-Mau». Une révolte paysanne et anti-coloniale en Afrique noire. 1971
2. M.L. Daneel: Old and New in Southern Shona Independent Churches. Volume I: Background and Rise of the Major Movements. 1971.
3. Network Analyses: Studies in Human Interaction. Edited by Jeremy Boissevain and J. Clyde Mitchell. 1973
4. M.L. Daneel: Old and New in Southern Shona Independent Churches. Volume II: Church Growth. Causative Factors and Recruitment Techniques. 1973

* *The Afrika-studiecentrum cannot in any way be held responsible for the views or opinions expressed in these books.*

Cover-design by Jurriaan Schrofer

Library of Congress Catalog Card Number: 73-91696

Printed in the Netherlands

To Nicole Grandin and Flora Petit

Acknowledgements

For the contents of this book I am very much indebted to the many Kenyans and people of other nationalities who gave me information during my stay in Kenya, most often during informal conversations held on Mau Mau or on general political topics. It is impossible to mention them all, but without their cooperation this book could not have been written.

As for the usage of the English language my thanks are due to my colleague Mr. Verney February who patiently tried to transform my special brand of Dutch English into good English. Professor J. Beattie of the University of Leiden made many valuable comments on a first draft of this book. Of course, only I am responsible for what I have written.

All photo's have been reproduced by kind permission of *Daily Nation Newspapers*, Nairobi.

Finally I wish to thank the Afrika-Studiecentrum for having enabled me to spend two months for study in Kenya.

Mau Mau: The men, the myth and the moment

A foreword by ALI A. MAZRUI

*Makerere University, Kampala and Center for Advanced Study
in the Behavioral Sciences, Stanford*

Rather apologetically, Dr. R. Buijtenhuijs chooses October 20, 1952 as the date of inception of the Mau Mau movement. This was the day of the declaration of the State of Emergency. The author rightly says that the origins of a movement such as this cannot be located so precisely and should certainly not be dated from the day the authorities against whom the movement was fighting finally realized that they had a problem on their hands. But given that specific date, the movement celebrated the twentieth anniversary of its birth on October 20, 1972.

What was the political picture of East Africa in October 1972? The historical background of East Africa's three presidents provided an interesting perspective on the regional significance of Mau Mau in history.

Kenya was presided over by Jomo Kenyatta, a man whom the colonial authorities had convicted on charges of helping to found and manage Mau Mau. At the head of affairs in Uganda was Idi Amin, a man who served on the side of the colonial forces within Kenya and participated in the attempt to suppress the movement. At the helm in Tanzania was Julius K. Nyerere, a man who shrank in horror from the violence of both sides in the 1950's, and who decided to encourage a nationalist movement based on non violence and moderation in contrast to the rebellion in Kenya. In other words, by the time Mau Mau was celebrating its twenthieth anniversary, three important perspectives on the movement were symbolized by the three presidents who together presided over the East African community.

But also captured in the picture of twenty years later were other dimensions of the total African experience. Amin, who had been a loyal soldier of the colonial authorities and had participated in the violent pursuit of Mau Mau fighters, was, by 1972, actively engaged in drastically reducing British influence and power in independent Uganda. Kenyatta was, by October 1972, much closer to the British in sympathy than the man across the border who had once helped to chase on behalf of the British desperate Kikuyu fighters. The Mau Mau movement had in part been inspired by a desire to break the disproportionate European presence in the rural economy of Kenya. Amin's expulsion of the Asians twenty years later was designed to break a disproportionate Indo-British dominance in the urban sector of Uganda's economy.

The struggle for indigenization in the economic affairs of East Africa over the last twenty years had revealed three dramatic events. Kenya's dramatic event was precisely the Mau Mau insurrection, a movement which released forces which ended the myth of the White Highlands and special prerogatives for white settlers, and thus terminated the presumptuous idea that Kenya was in some sense 'a white man's country'.

Uganda's great moment of dramatic economic indigenization was precisely the push which General Amin undertook in 1972 to terminate the Asian economic presence in Uganda, and drastically reduce the British presence by nationalizing a number of British firms. Both the Mau Mau movement and Amin's expulsion of the Asians were surgical operations, painful and fundamentally brutal. Whether both would be equally vindicated by history is a question which only history can answer, in the fullness of time.

As for Tanzania's great moment of economic indigenization, this came with the Arusha Declaration in 1967, nationalizing a number of industries in Tanzania and working out broad guidelines of a new national ethic. In the history of mainland Tanzania (Tanganyika) there have been fewer instances of brutal solutions than in either Kenya or Uganda. It was therefore in keeping with the more moderate historical background of Tanzania's political culture that the Arusha Declaration as a dramatic moment of indigenization was, in the final analysis, less brutal than either the Mau Mau insurrection or the wholesale expulsion of Asians from Uganda.

8

Of course Dr. Buijtenhuijs is not concerned in this book with either the Arusha Declaration or Amin's expulsion of the Asians as two companion events in the struggle to re-africanize Africa. But when placing the Mau Mau movement in historical perspective, a regional perspective is at times also relevant.

In writing about the fighters in the forest, there are two risks which authors run. One risk is not to see the wood for the trees. This happens when the individual events of the movement, or individual idiosyncracies of participants in the movement begin to obscure the broader social phenomenon which the whole revolt signified. Curiously enough, it has been pre-eminently the books written by former fighters in the Mau Mau movement which have quite often concentrated on the details at the expense of the general picture.

Academic writers tend to err in the other direction. They are so keen to place the Mau Mau movement in Kenya's general history that sometimes it is the trees which suffer. The wood acquires an overpowering independent presence. Carl Rosberg and John Nottingham, in writing *The Myth of 'Mau Mau'*, ended up writing the political history of Kenya.

Does Dr. Buijtenhuijs in this book commit a similar mistake? The balance is a little better in this book, though the book itself is not as substantial as the one by Rosberg and Nottingham, nor does it have for its background as extensive a knowledge of Kenya as that of Rosberg and Nottingham.

Another distinction between the two books is that Buijtenhuijs' is a book much more about contemporary Kenya than the work by Rosberg and Nottingham. The two books should perhaps be read together, for jointly they give a fascinating picture of the flow of Kenya's political history in relation to nationalistic and ethnic forces.

Buijtenhuijs' approach attaches considerable importance to images in human affairs, and sees a movement like Mau Mau as a great eruption of human paradoxes. The heroic and the mundane, the assertive and the timid, the rational and the confused, the effervescent and the insipid – all these contradictions manifested themselves in the men engaged in the Mau Mau movement, in the myths which animated them, and in the nature of that powerful moment in Kenya's history.

Was it all a peasant revolt? Inspite of the differences between Mzee Kenyatta and Chairman Mao, was the insurrection in Kenya comparable to the rural forces which led to Mao's triumph in China? There is certainly an element of genuine earthiness in both the movements, though the causes were not identical, and the consequences came to be significantly divergent. Much of the agitation behind the Mau Mau insurrection in Kenya was by people who were landless, living as squatters on European estates, and observing hungrily large tracts of land, either prosperously fertile or totally unused, all reserved exclusively for whites. As Donald L. Barnett put it in his introduction to Karari Njama's *Mau Mau From Within*:

'It is not only the brute fact of landlessness, land hunger and insecurity of tenure which conditioned the Kikuyu involvement in the nationalist movement and peasant revolt; it is also the fact that for a people who attach such sacred meaning to the land the areas alienated remained within their field of experience, unattainable yet in considerable measure unused by its new (white) owners.'*

The final outcome was the revolt of the rural dispossessed, and the long years of Kenya's State of Emergency. The white man's burden had proved to be too heavy a burden for the black peasants of the central lands of Kenya, and they were not prepared to carry it any further.

Was the Chinese peasant revolution a shadow across Kenya's peasant revolt? Certainly many of the white settlers of Kenya suspected communist instigation behind the Mau Mau insurrection, though because of Jomo Kenyatta's visit to the Soviet Union in the 1930's, this communist instigation was deemed to have come through Stalin's Russia rather than Mao's China. And yet, there were aspects of the Mau Mau phenomenon which betrayed at least a certain awareness of the Chinese model. The very name 'Mau Mau' has continued to have a touch of mystery about it. Jomo Kenyatta, when accused of founding the movement, was interrogated about the meaning of 'Mau Mau' in his trial at Kapenguria.

* Barnett and Njama, *Mau Mau From Within: Analysis of Kenya's Peasant Revolt* (New York and London: Monthly Review Press, 1967) p. 34.

He disclaimed any definite knowledge as to the significance of the term.

Another member of the movement who later became a member of the Kenya government was Josiah M. Kariuki. Kariuki wrote a book after his release from detention about his experiences as a Mau Mau detainee. Kariuki attributed the authorship of the name 'Mau Mau' to the *enemies* of the movement.

Rosberg and Nottingham wonder whether the name is a corruption of the Kikuyu word for 'oath'. I have also heard it speculated that the letters 'M.A.U.' were intended to be reversed to give the initials for 'Underground African Movement'. Why then were the initials reversed? To emphasize the ambition of reversing the scale of power in colonial Kenya, and to stress the *underground* nature of the movement. Why 'Mau Mau' twice over? 'For reasons of sound effect, and to echo the noise of a black cat in the stillness of the night.'

But political philologists will not let sleeping cats lie. They would still insist on exploring other theories of origin. Rosberg and Nottingham traced the name to 1948. That was the year of the critical initiation of the Chinese Revolution, prior to its ultimate culmination with the takeover in 1949. One of the leaders of the Mau Mau insurrection came to be called 'General China'. This was Waruhiu Itote. The outbreak of violence in Kenya coincided with the lingering Korean War. Harold C. Hinton in his book, *Communist China in World Politics*, suggestively refers to a 'General Korea' within the Mau Mau movement. The British were also involved at the time in fighting communist 'terrorism' in Malaya, similar to the 'terrorism' of the Mau Mau. Rosberg and Nottingham refer to the British application in Kenya of 'rehabilitation' methods based in part on their experience in fighting ethnic Chinese in Malaya.

Is it conceivable that the more sophisticated Kenya rebels had vaguely come to admire what the Chinese had been doing in both China and Malaya? Was that why Itote called himself 'General China'?

Did this sinophilia influence the name which finally emerged? Was the designation of Kenya's 'peasant revolt' a corruption of '*Mao Mao*' in honor of Mao Tse-Tung? Or was the name really forced upon the movement by others? Dr. Buijtenhuijs is right in discussing imagry as an important political reality in its own right. And images are at times captured in names, words, and their associations.

Intriguing also is Dr. Buijtenhuijs' discussion of images of Mau Mau in Kenya's corpus of creative literature. He laments the absence of 'resistance literature', strongly committed to the values of the Mau Mau movement and glorifying the activists within that movement. Buijtenhuijs is right in seeking broader sociological reasons for Kenya's ambivalence about the Mau Mau movement, both among writers and among political decision-makers. Dr. Buijtenhuijs has strong reservations about the attitudes and policies adopted by the Kenya government in relation to the former Mau Mau fighters. Some of these subjects within Kenya have been taboo for a while, but it is time that the debate about the meaning of Mau Mau for Kenya became a little more open. Dr. Buijtenhuijs' contribution may well turn out to be significant in that regard.

But while Buijtenhuijs and myself as scholars might be interested in greater openness of discourse, we should at least also bear in mind the special perspectives of politicians in an African situation. In the year of Kenya's independence I had occasion to refer in an article about Mau Mau to the French philosopher Ernest Renan who, in 1882, wrote an essay entitled 'What is a Nation?'–and then proceeded to observe that one essential factor in the making of a nation is 'to get one's history wrong'. In an exaggerated way Renan was making a basic point not only about successful nationhood, but also about successful marriage. The secret of successful marriage over a long span of time is to know what to forget. A couple has its ups and downs in the course of the relationship. Sometimes, in moments of anger, a couple may be profoundly cruel to each other. Sometimes incidents of shame, as well as of pain, occur to bedevil their domestic accord. If the couple were to remember all those unhappy occasions of pain, recrimination, cruelty, and shame, it would be surprising if the marriage survived for very long. But domestic love is a process of selection, emphasizing what is positive, playing down what is negative. What keeps a marriage afloat for more than a few years is, quite simply, the genius of selective amnesia.

The same considerations are at play in nation-building, and in relations between groups generally. Accord between these groups necessitates a cultivated ability to emphasize the positive aspects of their relationship, and to try to control and underplay the negative aspects. The Kenya government's handling of the Mau Mau myth has not been as consistent as this. There has been a fear of making the fighters too heroic, for this might conceivably have repercussions among those, especially in Kikuyuland, who have reason to resent some of the acts committed by the fighters during the Mau Mau movement.

Dr. Buijtenhuijs handles some of these issues with the paradox of tactful candour. He does address himself to the dimension of the Mau Mau movement which verges on being a civil war, and discusses the triumph of the movement in terms of subsequent political and economic stratification in Kenya.

The Mau Mau movement was militarily defeated by the British, but it was clearly a victory of the vanquished. The political triumph went to the African people, even if the military successes were retained by the colonial authorities. The Mau Mau movement was also the first great African liberation movement of the modern period. All the efforts which are now being made in southern Africa to consolidate resistance, and organize sabotage, and seek to dispel white power and privilege, have for their heroic ancestry that band of fighters in the Aberdare Forest of Kenya.

But did the right people in Kenya benefit from the movement? Were the rewards of political victory shared justly? Buijtenhuijs has reservations about the distribution of rewards, the allocation of credit, and the vindication of values. To him Kenya has retained some of the elements of injustice which characterized the regime against which the Mau Mau fighters directed their rustic weapons.

This book is stimulating, informative and irritating. That makes it worth reading. But it is also an important contribution to the literature on the Mau Mau movement.

13

Contents

15

Introduction

Today, as I write this introduction, it is exactly twenty years ago that a State of Emergency was declared in Kenya. Although a 'Mau Mau' *movement* (or should we say several 'Mau Mau' movements?) had already been in existence for some years, probably since 1947 or 1948, it is generally agreed that the 'Mau Mau' *revolt* started on the 20th October 1952, the day this State of Emergency was declared.

Today then would be an appropriate moment to ask a few questions about Mau Mau and to try to answer some of them. During the last five or six years some highly qualified scholars have published their research findings on the Mau Mau movement (D.L. Barnett and Karari Njama; C.G. Rosberg Jr. and J. Nottingham); at the same time some ex-freedom fighters (W. Itote; K. Muriithi; J. Wamweya) have recorded their life stories and, in doing so, shed more light on the Mau Mau revolt in general. Our scientific knowledge of the whole phenomenon has been greatly increased by these publications, and I myself have made extensive use of them in my thesis (1971). Although many questions on the central aspects of the whole movement as it existed from about 1948 till 1956 onwards remain unanswered even after this rich harvest of material, I feel that it would be premature to go into this subject once more. Thanks to the efforts of the History Department of the University of Nairobi more material and especially more life stories will soon be at our disposal, and only after the publication of these 'primary products' will historians be able to take up again the question of the deeper meaning and the essential characteristics of the Mau Mau movement.

There are, however, two closely related questions which have generally been neglected in the literature on Mau Mau and on which it is possible to comment today without waiting for new material. They do not bear directly on Mau Mau as a historical phenomenon but rather on present-day circumstances. The first could be formulated as follows: what today is the image of the Mau Mau revolt in historiography, in literature and in the public life of Kenya? From the material at our disposal a rather confusing and ambiguous, on some points even contradictory, image of the Mau Mau movement emerges. It is quite obvious that many people in Kenya have no clearly formulated idea about Mau Mau and do not know how to live with its memory. This certainly springs partly from the 'ambiguous' character of the Mau Mau movement itself,* but it is also related to some actual problems in Kenya politics. It is my aim here to study more thoroughly the image or images of Mau Mau and the factors that contributed to the making of these.

Another question automatically crops up in this context: what happened to the ex-freedom fighters and to the ex-detainees? What is their place in public life in Kenya and what special treatment, if any, did they receive from the Kenya Government since Independence? It is often suggested that the Mau Mau freedom fighters came off badly after Independence and that other people, not they themselves, reaped the fruits of *Uhuru*. However, most of the authors who adhere to this thesis are very parsimonious with exact data and figures. This then, is my second aim in writing this book: to gather some more concrete facts about the alleged neglect of the ex-freedom fighters and to see how far this problem plays a role in actual Kenya politics.

A few words about the way this study came into being are necessary. I was in Kenya for only two months (August and September 1971) and the main objective of my stay was to make a general study of the political life of the country since Independence. Scrutinising recent newspapers in order to inform myself on this subject, I found some very interesting news items and articles on Mau Mau today. As I had been working for years on a sociological

---

* This problem has been worked out in detail in my thesis: *Le Mouvement 'Mau Mau': Une révolte paysanne et anti-coloniale en Afrique noire*, The Hague – Paris, Mouton, 1971. See especially the Preface.

18

study of the Mau Mau movement which had then just been published, my interest in the whole phenomenon was revived. I then decided to collect, during my short stay in Kenya, as much data as I could on the problems of 'Mau Mau, Twenty Years After.' Back in Holland, I went through the existing literature in order to complete my information as far as possible.

I am well aware of the limitations of this approach, but almost nothing at all has been published on the whole subject, although it is quite important for Kenya, now and in the future. I am also aware that I pose more questions in this book than I am able to answer. I only hope that at least they are the right questions. If so I may hope to stimulate other people, preferably Kenyans, to try to answer them.

In that case I would have reached my goal of making a humble contribution to a better understanding by Kenyans of a very controversial but crucial period of their history.

Leiden, October 20, 1972   R.B.

1 Some Background Material: Kenya Politics, 1960-1972

A. Tribal politics

It is not my intention in this chapter to give a detailed, exhaustive and chronological analysis of political life in Kenya since independence, but rather to underline some important aspects of Kenya politics, especially in so far as they have or have had a special bearing on Mau Mau issues. For this reason, some very important factors in Kenya politics, for example, the personality and role of outstanding political leaders like Tom Mboya or Oginga Odinga, will not be treated at all or only in passing, while other factors will receive what at first may seem undue treatment. The justification for this disequilibrium will be found later on in the text.

The colonial legacy

'Tribalism' is undoubtedly one of the main factors that has played a role in Kenya politics all through the period considered here, and it is quite obvious that this situation is partly a consequence of events and policies dating from the colonial period, sometimes going back as far as the 1920s. In 1925 the colonial administration already authorized some African participation in political life by allowing Africans to become members and sometimes even elected members of the Local Native Councils. The LNC's, however, only existed on the district level, and no African was permitted to indulge in official politics on the national or even the provincial level, with the result that from that time on a tradition of locally based and tribally minded political parties became firmly established in

21

Kenya. After the Second World War national parties were allowed for a short period, but the Emergency in 1952 very soon resulted in a ban on all political parties. Again, when the ban was partially lifted in 1957, only district political associations were at first permitted. The result of this policy has been that Kenya, in the early sixties, was plagued by a profusion of regional political leaders, real kinglets in their own constituencies, but had only a few national leaders, a fact that seriously hampered the formation of national parties when they were again allowed in 1960.

KANU and KADU

After a great many difficulties two national parties were finally formed, the Kenya African National Union (KANU), representing an alliance between the Kikuyu, the Luo and the Kamba, the three biggest and politically most advanced tribes, and the Kenya African Democratic Union (KADU). There were no ideological differences in the real sense of the word between these two movements, KADU being mostly, if not exclusively, a reaction of the less advanced minority tribes, particularly the Kalenjin and the Coastal groups, against the menace of a domination by the 'big three' from KANU. In the words of E.W. Soja: 'KADU was a negative or "anti" party from the start, particularistic, and traditionally oriented. It lacked a dynamic program for nation building'.[1]

The land question was probably the fundamental issue dividing both parties.[2] The Kalenjin in particular, were very suspicious of the Kikuyu, both groups coveting the lands in the ex-White Highlands which the Kenya Government at that moment was buying from European farmers. In 1963 the situation in the Rift Valley was very tense indeed and even today the problems of the ex-White Highlands are far from being solved as we shall see in our fourth chapter.

Kenya thus entered the international scene with two parties, and, even more important, with two weakly structured and rather feeble parties. KANU, which was already the majority party before independence and which is actually the only political party in Kenya, never really succeeded in going beyond the stage of an alliance between different ethnic groups and different local interests. Consequently its role in national politics has been rather reduced. Mostly the party simply stayed dormant, exhibiting outbursts of

22

activity only at election times. In August 1971 a Kanu Reorganisation Committee presented a report on the renovation of the ruling party and recommended a complete overhaul of the party machinery. At this moment the party elections which must be held in order to implement the recommendations of the Reorganisation Committee are still in preparation. However it is already clear from press comments from the first half of 1972 that the big membership drive which was to be organized before the elections has been a partial failure and that the elections will probably not solve the fundamental problems of the party.

As far as KADU is concerned, it suffered from the same ills and weaknesses as its counterpart and it did not survive independence for long. During the period 1961–63, however, KADU played an important role in Kenya politics because it had the active support of substantial sections of the Asian and European population, while it represented only a minority of the African masses. With European and Asian support, the KADU leader Mr. R.G. Ngala, even had the honour to form the first internally autonomous government in Kenya and with the help of the Colonial Office the balance was weighted heavily in favour of KADU during the different negotiations leading to Kenya's Independence. Such was this weight that Kenya, in December 1963, found itself saddled with an extremely confused and complicated regionalistic Constitution meant to defend the rights of the minority tribes united in KADU.

The Kikuyu lead

We have seen that the tribalistic orientation of Kenya politics can be traced back partly to colonial policies concerning African political development. However, the ethnic antagonisms we mentioned are not just completely artificial creations springing from the divide-and-rule-policies of a Machiavellian colonial administration. They are also based on some hard facts, which it would be very difficult to set right in the near future, namely the considerable lead that a few ethnic groups enjoy over others both in the field of political consciousness and in that of economic and social development. This differential evolution started way back in the early 1920's, when the Kikuyu, and to a lesser degree the Luo and the Luhya, showed manifest signs of a rapid political awakening, while the other groups, in particular the pastoral tribes and the coastal

23

Bantu, did not. In 1960 this evolution had resulted in very sensible differences in the domain of modernisation and the integration in the political community. The fear of a Kikuyu – Luo domination which motivated the minority groups supporting KADU was thus not quite unfounded.

Since 1966 and certainly today, all fears of Luo domination have definitely been dispelled and the Luo have even joined the camp of those who feel and claim that they have lost out in the actual situation. The apprehension of an eventual Kikuyu domination, on the other hand, still does exist and is even much stronger than it was in the beginning of the 1960s. There are supporting facts which make this apprehension quite understandable. D. Rothchild who has made a very penetrating analysis of the problem of ethnic inequalities and imbalances in Kenya, begins his section on the 'facts of inequality' by saying that 'regional discrepancies in education... seem particularly significant in this regard, for they emphasize not only the priorities of the past but the resultant supply of manpower for the future'.[3]

He then provides a table on primary school enrollment and child population (children aged 7 to 13) by province in 1964 which shows a definite Kikuyu lead in education, the ratio for Central Province, the Kikuyu homelands, being 94.0% and for Nairobi, the Kikuyu-dominated capital, 137.3%, while the ratio for Kenya as a whole stood at 57.7%. Western Province with a primary school ratio of 70.6% was, in 1964, the nearest competitor to the Kikuyu areas.[4] A rather similar situation seems to exist in the field of higher education. During the debates on the University of Nairobi Bill in the National Assembly in July 1970 'some members went as far as alleging that 70% of the present intake comes from one province and belongs to one tribe and that the administrators in the college also come from one tribe'.[5] One of these members then asked, amidst cheers from some backbenchers, 'whether it was only the Kikuyu who could provide the country with qualified people'.[6] While there may be some exaggeration in the facts quoted in Parliament, it is certainly true that the Kikuyu dominate the University scene in Kenya, although the Luo also are well represented.

The same imbalances exist in the field of economic development. According to Rothchild again the statistics on the Industrial and Commercial Development Corporation loans up to April 1966

24

show that 64% of all the industrial loans and 44% of all the commercial loans went to Kikuyu, who only represent 20% of the male population.[7] After the European farmers were bought out, the Kikuyu also got 40% of the plots turned over to Africans in the ex-White Highlands although it is not sure that they as a group made a net gain here. Squatters who had previously been working on the large-scale European farms were frequently driven away when they did not belong to the tribe to whom the region was allocated and many of them happened to be Kikuyu. H. Ruthenberg who gives the most extensive data on this problem concludes that: 'It is open to question whether a comparison of the economic loss to the Kikuyu farm labourers, with the economic gain to the Kikuyu settlers, would reveal an economic gain for this tribe as a whole'.[8] According to this author the Kalenjin have been the big winners in the settlement-scramble.

It is no wonder that under these circumstances journalists and Members of Parliament of the non-Kikuyu groups regularly denounce the Kikuyu monopoly of jobs in certain sectors in particular or of top-level jobs in general. In 1970 the Kikuyu held in fact nine of the 22 permanent secretaryships, the highest non-political position in the Central Government administration, while four of the seven provincial commissioners were also Kikuyu.[9]

Other examples are numerous and, quite logically, people started whispering (or shouting!) about corruption and nepotism, or 'brotherization' as the Kenya terminology has it. Before we endorse these accusations, however, we must take one fact into account, formulated by S. Meisler as follows: 'The Kikuyu are the most educated, experienced, resourceful, energetic, adaptable and modern tribe in Kenya. If all promotions and appointments could be controlled strictly by an objective, computerized test of merit, the Kikuyus probably would still hold almost all the positions they have today.'[10]

We have seen that this is true as far as education is concerned. It is equally true in terms of energy, resourcefulness and dynamism: the Kikuyu indeed have proven all through history that they are a 'driven' people, typical 'achievers' in the sense of Mc Clelland, which is to be explained not in terms of inherent characteristics of the Kikuyu mind, but rather on the basis of a configuration of cultural and historical factors as I pointed out in my thesis (1971).

However, nepotism is certainly one of Kenya's main problems today and many Kikuyu who themselves have succeeded in life by their personal dynamism or because of their diplomas, later on have used their positions to help less-qualified or less-dynamic brothers or cousins. Many European and non-Kikuyu University staff members, for example, bitterly complain that non-Kikuyu do not have much chance to rise on the scientific ladder, while Kikuyu students sometimes manage to enroll for courses or seminars on the recommendation of some high-ranking official even after having failed the entrance examination. A similar situation exists in some ministries, and it has to be said here that the Kikuyu are not the only ones at fault. They only have more possibilities than the other tribes.

Of course the Kenya public is clearly aware of this problem as is shown by a public opinion poll held in 1968 in Nairobi City. On the question: 'Do you think that members of certain tribes are able to get jobs more easily than equally or even better qualified members of other tribes?', 58% of the interviewed answered 'yes', 20% said 'no', and 20% didn't know or refused to answer; 46% of the interviewed gave the Kikuyu as the most favoured tribe, 6% the Luo, 1% the Luhya and 5% other tribal groups.[11] This means that about 80% of the inhabitants of Nairobi who believe that nepotism and tribalism are a problem in Kenya, are convinced that its mechanism works especially in favour of the Kikuyu. This is an important factor in Kenya politics, and in this field the facts are often less important than what people think.

Government policy
It is of course quite difficult to say exactly what the Government policy is in these matters. In many cases, especially when it concerns practical and rather trivial matters, like the appointment of a driver or a messenger-boy, there is in a way no Government policy at all, individual Ministers, Permanent Secretaries, or District Commissioners deciding each on their own the 'policy' of their Ministry or Office. In so far as an official policy on ethnic inequalities does exist, Rothchild thinks that: 'The Government sought to reconcile development and equity; but, where a choice between the two was inescapable, it seemed ultimately to place greatest emphasis upon the nations' economic growth'.[12] Although Government spokesmen have always denied that there is any deli-

berate effort to favour the Kikuyu to the detriment of other ethnic groups, the Kenya Government, on the other hand, has refused to make use of tribal preferences or quotas in matters of employment and promotion,[13] which in practice means allowing the Kikuyu to take the full profit from their educational lead. It is difficult to see what the Government could have done otherwise in the private enterprise and private initiative society for which Kenya has opted right from the start. As Meisler puts it: 'It is nearly impossible to stem the drive of the Kikuyus. Moreover, it is doubtful whether the government of a developing country should make any attempts to dampen the enthusiasm of its most aggressive people. The drive of the Kikuyus is what development is all about.'[14] Meisler is quite right as far as capitalist development is concerned. For development on socialist lines other qualities are also necessary, but then this is clearly not Kenya's choice.

No separatism

There is, of course, a lot of disappointment and frustration in Kenya about the tribal aspects of Kenya politics, especially among members of the 'have-not' tribes. Nowadays even many Kikuyu are dissatisfied, because they aver that there is no danger of Kikuyu domination, but rather of Kiambu domination, Kiambu being one of the four Kikuyu districts, the one where President Kenyatta was born and where he still lives. It is very difficult to appraise the exact situation in this domain, but it is in fact quite clear that such a danger does exist on the level of national politics: Kiambu district is certainly over-represented in the Government and, to worsen matters, the few Cabinet-Ministers who have Kenyatta's ear and who form a sort of 'courtier' group at his Gatundu home are almost all from Kiambu District.[15]

However, the ethnic clashes and antagonisms that have plagued Kenya's political history from 1960 till today have never resulted in any separatist movement. The only exception have been the Somali *shifta's* of the North Eastern Province who for years have claimed the right to be re-united with their ethnic brothers in Somalia. Although the Kenya Government was given wide emergency powers over the North-Eastern Region at Independence, emergency powers which have still not been repealed, and although some hard fighting took place between Kenya military forces and the

Somali *shifta* in 1965–66, this separatist movement has remained a peripheral problem without any decisive influence on national politics in Nairobi.

For the rest the contest for power between the different ethnic groups of Kenya has always been a 'contest for power at the centre, not the periphery'.[16] That is, this has been so up till now. However, in a parliamentary debate on February 28, 1968, an Assistant Minister for Labour, Mr. Oselu-Nyalick, warned that 'if the present trends were not changed, Kenya might be headed towards 'another Biafra'.[17] It is always dangerous to accept declarations of this kind on face value, but many Kenyans and outside observers have gained the impression during the last few years that the official Government policy in Kenya has some particularistic and even parochial aspects. This can become dangerous for the country, especially when the problem of the succession of President Kenyatta becomes a reality. Kiambu cannot for ever 'rule the hills', just as Brittania has not been able to rule the waves indefinitely.

B. Class politics

Apart from tribalism and the fight against it, class politics have been an influential factor in Kenya politics since Independence. It can even be said that both factors – the class factor and the tribal one – are the poles between which Kenya's political pendulum has been swinging during the last twelve or thirteen years. Two periods can even be distinguished in Kenya's political history till 1972. Since independence, when the tribal factor was still clearly predominant as is shown in the existence of two – then tribal – parties, KANU and KADU, there has first been a gradual shift away from tribal politics towards class politics. This movement which had its high spots in November 1964 and again in the spring of 1966, more or less continued until the beginning of the summer of 1969. At that moment a drastic change took place in Kenya politics and the political pendulum sharply deflected again towards the tribal pole. Although it has swung back a little bit since, we have to admit that we are actually still definitely in the new 'tribal' period. But before we can go more thoroughly into this problem of the periodisation of Kenya's political history we will first have to analyze the facts on which class politics in Kenya are based.

28

The Swynnerton Plan and its effects

Class politics are of course based on the existence of social classes. In Kenya we can analyse the formation of social classes since the early 1950's on two different levels. First there is the grass-root level, that is, the rural areas that once constituted the African reserves. Here again, the socio-economic policy of the colonial administration has left a heritage which has heavily impeded the political development of Kenya, although the Kenya Government seems to have accepted it without questioning and has never tried to undo the work done by the preceding rulers. This heritage dates from the 1954–1960 period when the colonial government, in answer to the Mau Mau revolt, launched an agricultural reform known as the Swynnerton Plan. The plan had, first of all, a technical-economic aspect described by Mr. Carey Jones in the following terms:

'Its bases were twofold. The first was the change of land-ownership from customary tenure to individual freehold. This involved the enclosure and registration of existing rights and, where there was excessive fragmentation in over-populated areas, the sorting out of scattered fragments and their re-assembly in areas around the homestead in roughly the same proportions of the kind of land as was held before... The second base was the provision on these consolidated or enclosed farms of farm plans or lay-outs, with rotational schemes, the introduction of exotic, high-yielding livestock and of high-priced cash crops.'[18]

Mr. Carey Jones has described the whole project in the most enthusiastic terms, going even so far as to say that Kenya should inscribe the names of the European sponsors of the project on its roll of honour.[19]

No doubt the Swynnerton Plan had its technical and economic merits: Land fragmentation, in the Kikuyu areas and elsewhere, was an economic and social problem of the first order and litigation about land rights was a plague on which huge sums of money were spent by generally rather poor peasants who could ill afford to do so.[20] Undeniably the agricultural reform has done some good here, especially as far as the second point is concerned.

The project, however, also had a political facet and as such it was clearly an Emergency measure. As M.P.K. Sorrenson says: 'The final objective... was essentially political: land consolidation and registration (and the agricultural revolution that was to follow)

29

were expected to create a stable middle class built around the Kikuyu loyalists... Such a class, it was hoped, would be too interested in farming to be seduced by Kikuyu politicians into further subversion'.[21]

In the political domain the Swynnerton Plan, implemented with great haste in the Kikuyu tribal areas and then introduced, with varying success, in other regions, has not exactly achieved the goals envisaged by the sponsors.

Nevertheless it had some quite important consequences. First of all, while the whole process of land-consolidation did not *create* landless people (these were already in existence but, as tenants, they often cultivated pieces of land belonging to richer families), more then ever before the official registration of land titles defined sharply the exact position of each peasant. Moreover the consolidation of farms made it less probable for farmers to lease land to tenants as had been the practice with small plots far away from their homestead. In this way a polarization of rural 'haves' and 'have-nots' did occur. In the second place, the registration of land titles made it much easier to buy and sell land, with the result that a group of rich and wealthy farmers, a small landed gentry and not a mere rural middle class, as Sorrenson maintains[22], is now slowly emerging. The whole process implied in the Swynnerton Plan also greatly enhanced the concepts of private property and individual ownership of land, which in turn would make it much more difficult than before to introduce socialist policies in agriculture. The Kenya People's Union (KPU), the more radical opposition party, founded in 1966 and banned at the end of 1969, attempted in its political campaigns to appeal to Kenya's dispossessed, but it never really succeeded in reaching the numerically very important group of small farmers who are actually still more impressed by the fact of having obtained for the first time in their life an official land-title and who thus overlook the small size of their land which dooms them to a life of relative poverty.

The 'Black' Highlands

The group of small farmers was greatly increased during the period 1962–67 by what is known as the 'one-million acre scheme', that is the settlement of landless African peasants in parts of the Rift Valley and in the other parts of the White Highlands, where

European farmers were bought out with grants and loans provided by the British Government and some other agencies. According to the 1970 report from the Department of Settlement, more than 160,000 formerly landless people (about 35,000 families) had been settled, on completion of the one-million acre scheme.[24] It is quite typical of Kenya's socio-economic policy that no attempts were made to keep the European farms unimpaired or to work them as economic units on a cooperative or collective base. Oginga Odinga and Bildad Kaggia, the most important leaders of the KPU, made the desirability of this one of the party's political issues, but right from the start, the government of President Kenyatta has been in favour of small-peasant farming on an individual basis, thus perpetuating a colonial policy. It must in all honesty be said that the great majority of Kenyan peasants probably really wanted this. According to some information dating from 1968, the settlement schemes have proved also relatively successful from an economic point of view. J.M. Due, for example, concludes that 'in the areas where settlers have been on their plots for four years, production and sales have surpassed those of the former owners'.[25]

Political control and business interests

Social classes are emerging not only in the countryside at the grass-root level but also on the national level in the towns, especially in Nairobi, where a new elite, sometimes referred to in East Africa as the 'Wa-Benzi' ('those who own a Mercedes-Benz'), is rapidly making its presence felt. This new elite comprising mainly the 'political class', that is all who by their political or administrative position have access to the new wealth generated by the national economy, is numerically quite important in Kenya. 'Its middle and upper classes as measured by income distribution and high-level manpower surveys, are three to four times the size of Tanzania's', says D. Koff.[26] It is not only an important group numerically, but also an aggressive and omnipresent group that sees no objection to the intertwining of political control, business interests and large-scale land ownership. Its members apparently do not fight shy of publicity nor are they discreet about their activities. In this they are encouraged by Kenya's political leaders.

President Kenyatta, in fact, is himself one of the best examples of this new elite.

Since 1961 he has become the owner of huge farms, and he apparently knows how to make them productive. 'I am myself a farmer,' is his favourite remark when opening one of the numerous Agricultural Shows that are part of Kenya's folklore. One can even say that, barring a few Europeans, he is probably Kenya's 'first farmer'. There is no doubt that he considers this situation to be quite normal, as is shown by the 'dialogue' he had in April 1965 with Bildad Kaggia, his co-detainee during the Emergency, at a political meeting in Murang'a. At that time Kaggia was a staunch critic of Kenya's social and agricultural policies. After having accused him of 'advocating for free things', Kenyatta went on: 'But we were together with Paul Ngei in jail. If you go to Ngei's home, he has planted a lot of coffee and other crops – what have you done for yourself? If you go to Kubai's home, he has a big house and a nice shamba – Kaggia what have you done for yourself? We were together with Kungu Karumbu in jail, now he is running his own busses – what have you done for yourself?'[27]

Many ministers, members of parliament and top civil servants have thus acquired substantial properties. Regular complaints are lodged in Parliament about this but no one seems to harbour any feelings of guilt. 'Am I the only Minister in this country doing business?', exlcaimed Mr. Angaine, the Minister of Lands and Settlement, when questioned in Parliament about his commercial interests.[28] He certainly is not, one of his colleagues being for a time even known as 'Mr. 10 percent' as a tribute to his business acumen. Even radical members of Parliament, like Mr. J.M Kariuki, who try to be champions of the poor, are themselves often big farmers and 'capitalists'.[29]

As far as I have been able to ascertain, Odinga seems to have aptly described the general feeling in Kenya that, 'we are getting a new class of Blundells, Delameres, and Briggs, deliberately created'[30] and that the rich are getting richer and the poor are getting poorer. This last point, however, is implicitly denied by D.P. Ghai in his contribution to *Zamani* where he argues that 'there is little doubt that impressive progress has been made throughout East Africa in promoting greater economic equality in recent years'.[31] Although Mr. Ghai does not provide much quantitative data to support his thesis, his article contains at least some interesting indications, particularly on agricultural development, which show that some times even the poor in Kenya do enjoy increases in wealth. His observations refer to the poor peasants, but not to the landless, who are growing in numbers and who form one of the biggest problems in Kenya today.

Right and left wings in KANU

Quite logically the existence of social classes or protoclasses in Kenya has led to the emergence of ideological themes in the political life of the country. Ideological differences were already in existence in KANU right from its inception in 1960, but up till 1964 the need to maintain, at least outwardly, the unity of the party in the struggle against the colonial administration and later on against the KADU opposition had prevented these differences from coming into the open. However, when the KADU leaders, realising that the battle for regionalism was a lost one, voluntarily dissolved their party in November 1964 and joined the KANU majority, the need for secrecy was no longer there. There is no doubt that the dissolution of KADU was a 'sign of maturity in the evolving polity and an indication of increasing interaction between the Kenyan equivalents of the "haves" and "have-nots".[32] It had not only the effect of making the need for internal unity inside KANU less evident; the influence in KANU of a group of rather pragmatic and tribally thinking ex-KADU politicians also considerably reinforced the conservative wing in the Party.

From that time onwards two factions were openly at war with each other in KANU, a 'moderate' one led by the trade union 'boss' Tom Mboya, the ex-KADU leaders and some Kikuyu politicians close to Kenyatta, and a 'radical' one, led by the Luo leader Oginga Odinga and Bildad Kaggia. Four issues, basically, divided these two groups. The first one was related to foreign affairs, Mboya and his friends wanting to maintain close ties with England without at the same time neglecting the friendship with the United States, while the radical group wanted to create political openings with China and the Eastern bloc. The following two points were connected with economics: the radicals wanted to nationalize certain industries and the most important public services, while the moderates tended to favour private enterprise everywhere; the radicals wanted to distribute free land to the landless taking it

33

eventually from the European farmers without compensation, while the moderates were in favour of buying the European farms and letting the new African smallholders in turn pay for the land. The last point touched social development: the radicals asked for free medical care and free education, as had been promised in the 1963 KANU programme while the moderates considered these promises incapable of being honoured yet for obvious budgetary reasons.[33]

The Kenya People's Union

During 1965 it gradually became clear that President Kenyatta, in spite of his old political friendship with Odinga, secretly inclined towards the moderates which gave new strength to the Mboya – Ngala – Njonjo coalition. Probably by the end of that year a decision was reached by the moderates to force the radicals to retreat or to withdraw from the party.[34] The real trial of strength came in March 1966 during the KANU Conference at Limuru, which seems to have been organized with the help and financial aid of the US Embassy in Nairobi.[35] Here the office of Vice-President of the Party, held at that moment by Odinga, was abolished. The other representatives of the radical KANU-wing also lost their positions on this occasion which led to their leaving the Party, and founding, after an interval of a few weeks, a new movement, the Kenya People's Union.

One might well ask whether this new party signified a reinforcement of the tribal element in Kenya politics or rather of the ideological, class-orientated element? Probably both. On the national level KPU proclaimed itself the party of the losers, the dispossessed, and it strongly attacked the new bourgeoisie which allegedly dominated KANU. Bildad Kaggia, opposing his fellow Kikuyu Kenyatta in the name of the poor, was certainly the most genuine representative of this tendency in KPU. In the subsequent elections in his Kandara constituency, however, he suffered a crushing defeat from his KANU opponent who very openly played upon Kikuyu solidarity. 'Kaggia, you have taken an uncircumcised spouse', sang the Kikuyu women at the political meetings in Kandara, a plain allusion to Kaggia's alliance with the Luo who do not practise circumcision.

34

In Luo-land, where the majority of the adherents of the new party were to be found, KPU represented first of all a tribal movement. Most of the Luo clearly did not bother too much with ideological problems, but were merely closing their ranks behind their tribal leader, who, they thought, had been ousted from KANU not because he was a radical but because he was a Luo. The fact that Odinga and the other Luo Members of Parliament who joined KPU were re-elected with a majority of 90% or more of the vote, certainly does not mean that all Luo at that time considered themselves as 'have-nots' compared to the other ethnic groups in Kenya.

However, KPU never really had an opportunity to carry the ideological debate to the national political scene. During the 'Little General Elections' in the summer of 1966, only those parliamentarians who had joined KPU were obliged to seek re-election which made it impossible to have a real 'count' of the sympathies of the Kenyan masses. Moreover, after these elections everything was done by the incumbent party to belittle KPU and to impede and undermine its growth. In the National Assembly, where KPU with its seven Members was too small to merit recognition as an official opposition party, the new radical group did to a certain extent benefit from a sort of gentlemen's agreement which allowed its members to speak freely on all actual political problems.

However, the agreement did not go beyond this limited arena. President Kenyatta himself reacted very violently against the new opposition party and in several public speeches he compared the members of the opposition with snakes that should be crushed without mercy.[36]

When, in June 1967, he bestowed high distinctions upon the political leaders who were his co-detainees during the Emergency, Achieng Oneko and Bildad Kaggia, who had joined KPU, were excluded from these honours.

On the practical side, several rather harsh measures were taken to upset KPU's political campaigns. 'Party functionaries were not permitted to hold public meetings anywhere in Kenya; second-echelon KPU officials were detained; in some cases, individual KPU members were physically attacked and party branch offices closed down by KANU activists.'[37] At the same time scarcely veiled hints were levelled at potential KPU sympathizers by, among others, outstanding Government leaders like vice-president arap

35

Moi who, at the end of 1967, 'warned the people at a country meeting that those who had received land under settlement schemes should 'support and co-operate with the government, otherwise their land might be taken back'.'[38] This intimidation campaign found its culminating point during the summer of 1968, when, a few weeks before the local government elections where about 1900 municipal and district councillors seats were at stake, the nomination papers of all KPU candidates were declared null and void on the grounds that they had been incorrectly filled in.[39] As no KANU candidate suffered the same fate it was quite clear then that KPU stood no chance ever to come to power legally.

Tribal politics again
During the second half of 1969 some dramatic events shook Kenya. They finally led to a reinforcement of tribal elements in all fields of public life and to a partial suppression of the ideological debates, which were being waged since the end of 1964.

It all started with the assassination of Tom Mboya, then Minister for Finance and Planning, on the fifth of July 1969. Mboya, a Luo himself, had always been a non-tribal urban leader, and he was the only Member of Parliament elected in a constituency (Nairobi-East) where his own tribe represented but a minority of the electorate. A staunch enemy of Oginga Odinga, Mboya had never had much Luo support during his political career. After his death, however, he became a sort of Luo hero and martyr, and the Luo people, who quite openly accused some leading Kikuyu politicians of instigating the murder, now more than ever rallied behind Odinga. Cries of 'war to the Kikuyu' were heard at Mboya's funeral in Nyanza, and President Kenyatta's car was stoned when he was on his way to a memorial service in the Cathedral of Nairobi.

In their turn, the Kikuyu reacted by closing their ranks in view of an eventual showdown. Only a few weeks after the death of Mboya, rumours were rife in Nairobi and elsewhere that thousands of Kikuyu were taking nocturnal oaths, swearing that they would see to it that the flag of Kenya never left the 'House of Mumbi' (i.e. the Kikuyu tribe). At the same time, in August 1969, Bildad Kaggia, the only outstanding non-Luo leader in KPU, suddenly announced his decision to leave the party and to rejoin KANU. By this decision, Kaggia gave a plain hint that even for him, tribal solidarity ultimately counted more than the class struggle, although he justified his volte-face by saying that if he stayed with the KPU he would never be able to play a constructive role in Kenya politics.[40]

Quite possibly the truth is somewhere in between but there can be no doubt that Kaggia's departure was a serious blow to KPU in so far as it made it wellnigh impossible for its leaders to continue pretending theirs was a non-tribal party. The party did, as a matter of fact, not survive long after Kaggia's resignation, although its disappearance from the political scene was not directly caused by it. In October 1969 President Kenyatta went to Nyanza to open a new hospital. Some unkind references to Odinga provoked hostile cries from the crowd and probably some menacing gestures. Kenyatta's bodyguards, thinking themselves in real danger, immediately opened fire, killing at least nine persons according to official sources, and many more, according to non-official eye-witnesses. Did Kenyatta deliberately provoke the Luo crowd and was it all designed to trap the KPU? It is rather difficult to answer this question, but it is certain that the Government has used the Kisumu disturbances as a pretext for banning the Kenya People's Union and sending its leaders into detention. At the same time, this meant a last blow to any endeavours to establish the paramountcy of class politics over tribal politics in Kenya's public life.

The general elections and the return to calm

The tensions which had accumulated during the second half of 1969 had for a great part dissipated in the beginning of 1970, mostly as a result of the parliamentary elections of December 1969 and January 1970. It may, at first sight, seem rather undemocratic to hold general elections just one month after the banning of the only opposition party, but it must be said that the Government did everything to provide the electorate with a real choice. This was done by instituting 'primary elections' within KANU in which any one was allowed to vote who gave a verbal declaration of support to the ruling party and in which anybody could stand as a candidate who was a paid up member of KANU for at least six months before the elections. Exceptions to this rule were made for civil servants and, with special permission from Mr. Kenyatta, for... some ex-KPU members like Bildad Kaggia and Mrs. Grace Onyango,

37

a close lieutenant of Oginga Odinga. In these elections about 62% of the former Members of Parliament were defeated including five Ministers and 14 Assistant Ministers,[41] probably a much higher percentage than it would have been had the elections been held under the former two-party system. This certainly had a 'cathartic effect',[42] especially in the Luo areas where all 'Government' candidates were heavily defeated and where Mrs. Onyango was elected in triumph. The result of this was that in March 1971 the Kenya Government felt strong enough to release Mr. Odinga and most of the other detainees of the defunct KPU. In September 1971, Mr. Odinga even rejoined KANU, which means that the risk of an imminent Kikuyu – Luo war is now over, at least for the moment.

C. Some institutions

At the end of this chapter some political institutions must be briefly analyzed because their role and their relative importance in the political life of Kenya, directly or indirectly, have been of influence on the manner in which problems relating to Mau Mau have been handled and solved since independence. This discussion will be selective and not all the political institutions of Kenya will be dealt with.

A critical Parliament

The pages devoted to the Parliamentary Debates are without any doubt among the most interesting and readable parts of the Kenya newspapers and they are indispensable for anybody who wants to get a clear picture of what is going on in the country. Right from the beginning of this century Kenya has had a Legislative Council that included people who were opposed to the official policy of the colonial administration and who were not afraid to say so. During most of the colonial period this opposition generally reflected more conservative viewpoints than those of the administration, Africans being excluded from the Legislative Council until 1944, but since the Second World War and especially since 1957 the opposition has been African and radical. In both cases the colonial government used to accept the most violent and passionate criticism without faltering...and most of the time without paying much attention either.

This tradition of a legislative council shaped into a 'critical, active, hardhitting body'[43] has been taken up anew by the Government of independent Kenya. Even today the honourable Members of Parliament often air their grievances and frustrations in no uncertain terms although they always refrain from direct attacks on President Kenyatta himself. The following is an example from the recent debate on the Emergency regulations still in force in the North-Eastern Province since the *shifta* war. During these debates one of the members dared to qualify the regulations as 'the most primitive of laws – worst than apartheid as practised in South Africa',[44] without being called to order by the Speaker.

It is also interesting to note that both during the days of the KADU opposition and those of the KPU, some of the most violent and persistent criticisms of Government policies did not come from the parliamentary opposition, but from KANU backbenchers. These KANU backbenchers have clearly always considered themselves as an 'opposition from within' having the duty to 'harass our own Government democratically', in order to keep 'the party's democratic machinery alive', as one of them declared in an article in the *Daily Nation*.[45] Some of the most important planks in the defunct KPU platform like the free allocation of land to the poor and enforcement of a limit on the amount of landed property that can be owned by a private person, still find their advocates among the now sitting MP's.

It is, however, quite difficult to say what exactly has been the influence of Parliamentary criticism on the Kenya Government. According to Ghai and Mc. Auslan:

'Doubts (...) remain of the real influence of the members. There are issues, like electoral laws, land and Africanization, where the back-bench opinion does appear to have influenced policy, but on many other issues the impression is gained that the Government ignores the views expressed in the Assembly.'[46] Ch. Gertzel essentially comes to the same conclusion when she states that 'the Government certainly overruled the backbenchers more often than they conceded their point'.[47] In 1970 an American scholar said about Nairobi University that 'possible academic dissent is channeled and allowed to harmlessly dissipate'.[48] The same might be true of Parliament which, like Parliaments elsewhere, often seems to be used only as a convenient instrument to blow off steam, rather than an effective policy-making institution.

A strong executive

The tradition of a strong and critical Parliament, in fact, runs counter to the equally well established tradition of a strong Government. This again is a colonial heritage. Of old, the colonial governors were real 'viceroys', extremely powerful and heading an omnipresent administrative machinery at all levels. In Kenya the necessities of the Emergency had reinforced this tradition even more, and at Independence it was perpetuated by the Kenyatta Government, especially as a means to combat the regional powers provided for in the first Constitution.

Since Independence the powers of the Executive have been reinforced even more, especially at the provincial and district level where the Provincial and District Commissioners preside *ex officio* on the many economic and development boards and committees that have come into existence during the last ten years. During this process the Members of Parliament have lost quite a bit of their influence and they are now in constant conflict with the administrators and civil servants on whom they are dependent for the licences necessary for holding public meetings... even in their own constituencies.[49]

Quite recently this conflict briefly came into the open when Members of Parliament unexpectedly complained of having been 'humiliated' during the official function marking the celebration of Kenyatta Day 1971 in Nairobi. Apparently there had not been sufficient seats on the official platform and some MP's were forced to stand under the blazing sun while top civil servants were comfortably seated in the shadow. The Speaker judged this event of sufficient weight to suspend the current debates, and one of the members, Mr. Charles Rubia, himself an Assistant Minister, very well summed up the general consensus of opinion when he stated that, 'it was time to decide whether the country was being run by civil servants or politicians'.[50] In fact, this decision seems already to have been taken quite a few years ago. As Ghai and McAuslan put it: 'When civil servants license political meetings, run local and other elections, co-ordinate the distribution of maize during shortages, oversee the land consolidation programs... it is obvious that the Government is in a position to control directly and in great detail most of what goes on in the country in the political, economic and social spheres, and ensure that developments in all these spheres contribute towards the consolidation of its position.'[51]

A divided Army?

In June 1971 announcements about the discovery of a plot to over-throw the legal government made the headline-news in Kenya and caused sensation all over the country. The details of the *coup* and especially the deeper meaning the conspirators wanted to give to their enterprise have never been fully disclosed, but it appears to have been an essentially Kamba-dominated affair, Major-General Ndolo, the then Chief of Defence Staff, being one of the principal plotters in the background.[52] This is not amazing if one recollects that the colonial army in Kenya has traditionally mainly found its recruits among the Kamba, who today still largely control positions of responsibility in Kenya's armed forces. In order to nip eventual Kamba inspired army *coups* in the bud the Kenya Government has already been trying for some time to come to an enforced 'crash-programme' to Kikuyuise the Army, and it is quite possible that some Kamba generals, like Ndolo, have tried to jump the gun before the young Kikuyu captains and lieutenants definitely replace them. The new Army Commander, Major-General Mulinge, is still a Kamba and the Kenya Army, like African armies everywhere, is still a political force to be reckoned with. However, a tribal equilibrium is gradually being built up in the armed forces,[53] and the fact that the General Service Unit and the Police are under Kikuyu command may also further restrain Kamba generals from staging another coup.

This, finally, would point to a less conspicuous role of the Kenya Army in politics as opposed to what has happened in some other African countries. One is however left with the rather difficult question of who will guard the guardians? In other words, who will eventually restrain the Kikuyu military leaders from political adventures once they have taken over the positions of power within the Army?

41

2 The Myth of Mau Mau in Public Life and in Historiography

> 'Toute société éprouve le besoin de transcrire en légendes certains faits de son histoire, de masquer certaines réalités sous des croyances.'[1]

A. Introduction

In 1954, Sir Philip Mitchell, Governor of Kenya from 1944 until June 1952, expressed his feelings on Mau Mau in the following way: 'That persons of some education... should describe this monstrous, nauseating wickedness as a "resistance movement" is intolerable – unless of course they mean a resistance movement against God and decency and morality and indeed everything that distinguishes man from the carrion-eating reptiles.'[2] Right from the start, Mau Mau evoked passions that have rarely been equalled in the history of the decolonization of the African continent. Therefore much of what has been written on the subject has been coloured by myths. Roughly speaking one can distinguish two myths pertaining to the Mau Mau, which are diametrically opposed and with each stemming from one of the two groups that have fought each other during the Emergency: the white settler and administrator community and the more radical sections of the Kikuyu people.

The European myth

Between October 1952 and the beginning of the 1960's, when Kenya entered the last phase of its decolonization process, the colonial administration and the settlers enjoyed an almost complete monopoly of the means of communication and of publicity. They have used this monopoly to impose their myth of the Mau Mau, a myth which is still extremely powerful in Europe and elsewhere and which makes it still quite difficult to comprehend fully the whole phenomenon. Although this myth had, of course, several variants, and although some individual Europeans adopted rather different standpoints during the Emergency, I will not go into this matter here, partly for lack of space but mainly because the European myth of Mau Mau as described hereafter was largely dominant and without doubt determined the official answer to Mau Mau.

The point of departure of the European myth is the hypothesis that the Mau Mau movement was not the culmination of a whole series of real and objective political and economic grievances, but the result of a profound mental instability 'springing from the abrubt collision of two civilizations'.[3]

Even the psychologist J.C. Carothers defends this thesis. After having summed up a certain number of 'objective' political and economic grievances of the Kikuyu population he goes on to say, finally, that the Mau Mau movement arose from an 'anxious conflictual situation in people who, from contact with the alien culture, had lost the supportive and constraining influences of their own culture, yet had not lost their "magic" modes of thinking'.[4]

If one accepts this psychological interpretation of the causes of the Mau Mau movement, one is also almost automatically led to a specific interpretation of the deeper meaning of the revolt. Mr. Lyttelton, the Secretary of State for the Colonies in 1952, was quite logical when he declared at a press conference in November 1952 that the Mau Mau revolt 'is not the direct child of economic conditions and *is not intended or designed to improve them*'.[5] In this way the belief came into being that Mau Mau stood for regression, for a return to the past. This thesis has been forwarded amongst others by the very official Parliamentary Delegation to Kenya which concluded in its report to the Secretary of State for the Colonies that 'Mau Mau intentionally and deliberately seeks to lead the Africans of Kenya back to bush and savagery, not forward into progress'.[6]

One finds this thesis with surprising regularity in the declarations and writings of people from quite different walks of life and belonging to quite distinct currents of opinion like, for example, Sir Michael Blundell, official spokesman of the moderate Kenya settlers ('Mau Mau is an atavist desire to get rid of civilisation, with all its restraints and discipline'),[7] John Brom, a reporter travelling to Kenya in search of sensation and strong emotions ('The Mau Mau adherents have shown... that they are only an

African secret sect, without any ideals and lacking a humanitarian basis'),[8] Margery Perham, outstanding expert on African affairs and generally favourably disposed towards African emancipation movements ('a revival ... of a corrupted savagery'),[9] and even social scientists like J. D. de Roock and M. Stanley, who saw in the Mau Mau revolt a 'counter-acculturation' movement, the result of a failure of the Kikuyu to adapt themselves to Western civilization.[10]

This 'regression' model of the Mau Mau is still widely believed in, explicitly or implicitly, as is shown in a study on African businessmen, published by P. Marris and A. Somerset in 1971: 'Businessmen deeply committed to the Mau Mau movement later accepted as a model *the civilization they had so stubbornly resisted.*'[11]

In his penetrating analysis of Mau Mau historiography O.W. Furley rightly makes a distinction between the 'official' version of Mau Mau (government reports and documents) and the 'missionary' interpretation of Mau Mau, although he admits that the differences between the two variants are only of minor importance.

The Kenya missionaries put a special emphasis on the religious struggle they thought was going on in Kenya and systematically presented this struggle as a fight between the forces of darkness and the forces of light. 'Missionary accounts of the history of the fight against Mau Mau', says Furley, 'almost give it the character of a East African crusade, to win back the Holy land which the missions had planted in Kikuyuland; a fight which produced its own saints and martyrs.'[12] This crusade aspect of the missionary interpretation of Mau Mau has been very well voiced in the following prayer used by the members of the Church Missionary Society in England: 'Finally let us pray: For the leaders and members of Mau Mau and for those who are under arrest; that they may be released from the power of darkness and set their faces towards the light.'[13]

It should not be thought, however, that this interpretation of Mau Mau was exclusively adhered to by missionaries. In 1960, Sir Patrick Renison, the then Governor of Kenya, still called Kenyatta, the presumed leader of the Mau Mau movement, 'a leader to darkness and death', and Sir Philip Mitchell, one of his predecessors, was even more outspoken in his Memoirs when he evoked: '... The black and blood-stained forces of sorcery and magic, stirring in the vicious hearts and minds of wicked men and, as the churches and

45

the schools speak over the land, whispering to them "Kill, kill, kill, for your last chance in Africa is at hand" ... The light is spreading, and these dark and dreadful distortions of the human spirit cannot bear it.'[14]

In summing up one may say that Kenya's white minority has presented the Mau Mau revolt more as a collective mental illness than as a rational political movement and that the British official answer to the revolt, placed under the sign of the 'rehabilitation' of the Kikuyu people, was an expression of this fundamental belief that Mau Mau was a dangerous mental illness having nothing to do with politics, nationalism or economic exploitation.

The African myth

For about ten years the European myth of Mau Mau practically went unchallenged, although it has to be said that a few European writers, especially from England, quite early in the Emergency period, presented a relatively more balanced view of the revolt. This is true in particular of D.H. Rawcliffe who, in 1954, said that Mau Mau was an 'incredible blend of political idealism, pagan savagery, and witchcraft. It is a paradox that the atrocities of Mau Mau have their origin in the urge towards enlightenment which is now surging through the vast African Continent – in its fusion of nationalism and primitive superstition Mau Mau has made its own unique contribution to the psychodynamics of revolution.'[15] Rawcliffe is far in advance of other writers of his time, and, in fact, quite close to some current interpretations of Mau Mau. He remained, however, an isolated case, and his terminology ('pagan savagery') still shows the influence of the European myth.

The real attack on the European myth of Mau Mau, in which African nationalists played a prominent part, came only much later. Since 1963, these nationalists have been trying hard to justify themselves, to undo the 'savage' image of the Mau Mau revolt created by the settlers and their allies, and to 'rehabilitate' the movement, not in the sense which the colonial rulers gave to this word, but in the real sense of the term. In doing this, they have in turn spawned a new myth, the African myth of Mau Mau.

Three books are of particular importance here. The first is '*Mau Mau*' *Detainee* by J.M. Kariuki, published in 1963. Here, for the first time, a Kenya African, who had been a member of Mau Mau himself, although not a forest fighter, took the floor and presented his version of the Emergency events. With Kariuki the whole picture changes: instead of 'bestialities' and 'savage crimes', he tells us of the 'heroic struggle' in the forest; instead of describing Mau Mau as a tribal movement he evokes 'the spirit of African nationalism of which we were a part',[16] and although he admits that the Mau Mau movement was led and manned principally by Kikuyu he insists on the fact that members of other tribes did take part in the revolt;[17] instead of analyzing Mau Mau as a 'return to the bush' and to the tribal past, he claims that it was a modern and rational political movement. The Mau Mau revolt, as pictured by Kariuki, does not differ much from the wars of liberation in Algeria or in Vietnam; the only difference is that the material means at the disposal of the Kenya freedom fighters were less modern and less important.[18]

Kariuki's book was still mostly a factual account of his own experiences in several detention camps in Kenya during the Emergency and the African myth of Mau Mau only appears 'in filigrane' and incidentally in his writings. The myth was, however, soon developed and scientifically enshrined by C. G. Rosberg Jr. and J. Nottingham. After having refuted the European thesis that the Mau Mau revolt was the consequence of the Kikuyu's failure to adapt to the modern world, these authors state that: 'In our view, the outbreak of open violence in Kenya in 1952 occurred primarily because of a European failure rather than an African one; it was not so much a failure of the Kikuyu people to adapt to a modern institutional setting as it was the failure of the European policy-makers to recognize the need for significant social and political reform. In suggesting that the European conception of "Mau Mau" constituted a myth, we maintain that "Mau Mau" was indeed an integral part of an ongoing, rationally conceived nationalist movement.'[19]

Rosberg and Nottingham, in their book, present a very systematic, complete and penetrating survey of the history of Kenya and of Kikuyu politics since the first world war, and their analysis of the roots of the Mau Mau *movement* will probably remain a standard work for a long time. However, they say practically nothing about the Mau Mau *revolt* and even less about the more controversial and 'disturbing' aspects of it. For this reason, and in spite of its very scientific and rather unbiased account of the Mau Mau pre-history, I feel that '*The Myth of* " *Mau Mau*" ' itself also belongs partially to a myth, the African one. It is, in fact, unscientific, given the actual stand of the debates on the problem, to write a book of about 350 pages on Mau Mau without even mentioning the so-called 'advanced oaths'. One can try to prove that they only existed in the imagination of slightly neurotic Europeans or that they were only used by the 'lunatic fringe', a tiny minority of the Mau Mau free-dom fighters. Yet it does not increase one's credibility to remain completely silent on the problem. This is even more true in the case of C.G. Rosberg who, in an earlier publication with G. Bennett, still accepted some elements of the European myth of Mau Mau, as is shown by the following quotation: 'To the gangs themselves Mau Mau was a freedom movement. It assailed the whole Europe-an position, both government and settler, whilst depending for its strength on *intimidation through bestial oathing* which made the movement all the more repugnant to Europeans.'[20]

It was a third author, W. Itote (ex-General China), who brought the African myth of Mau Mau to its logical conclusion in a book that appeared in Nairobi in 1967. Mr Itote has been the first im-portant forest-fighter (he led the Mau Mau Mount Kenya armies for more than a year) to write his memoirs and the first to give a detailed account of the life and struggle of the forest fighters as seen by an African nationalist.[21] Like Rosberg and Nottingham, he claims that Mau Mau was part of a modern nationalist movement, but he goes farther than this bare statement and takes up all the accusations that have been brought up against the Mau Mau fighters, trying to refute them one by one.[22] Quite a few Kikuyu seem to consider his book as the 'official' history of the Mau Mau revolt, and it certainly is an important document, although the difference between fact and fancy is not always easy to establish in the course of Mr. Itote's story. The three books we have mentioned here without doubt have had a great impact on the Kenya public with the result that many Kenyans today are inclined to believe in the African myth of Mau Mau and think of the revolt in terms of 'the Kenya War of Liberation' or 'the Kenya Revolution', as A.A. Mazrui predicted would happen.[23]

B. The 'Euro-African' myth

Today there are two elaborately constructed myths of Mau Mau, a European and an African myth. The European myth held sway unchallenged in historiography and in the public life of Kenya all during the colonial period. Therefore it would have seemed quite appropriate and logical for the African myth of Mau Mau to take over this unchallenged position after Independence. This was the evolution forecast for the immediate future by the anonymous author of 'La dialectique d'un mythe africain'.[24] It certainly would have been an intellectually and even 'aesthetically' satisfactory solution. However, the dialectics of the Myth of Mau Mau have been even more subtle than was ever dreamt of by this author.

In fact, during the period 1961–63 a third version of the Mau Mau revolt gradually came into being and it is this version that has succeeded the European myth, at least in Kenyan public life. This version of Mau Mau is not really a fully-fledged theory and it has never been worked out in writing. Nevertheless it certainly does exist and still forms one of the background themes in Kenya politics. Although not very clearly formulated, it basically has two sides. First of all it has borrowed some very important elements of the European version of Mau Mau, in particular the idea that Mau Mau was something 'obnoxious', something abnormal and to be ashamed of. President Kenyatta very bluntly expressed this idea in a speech given at a meeting in Githunguri in September 1962, where he went on record with the following statement: 'We are determined to have independence in peace, and we shall not allow hooligans to rule Kenya. We must have no hatred towards one another. *Mau Mau was a disease which had been eradicated, and must never be remembered again.*'[25]

Although this is by far the most outspoken condemnation of the Mau Mau movement I have come across in the writings and speeches of Mr. Kenyatta, it is certainly not the only one. While some others may be less explicit, they are nevertheless quite clear, as is evident from his answer in April 1961 to the question of why oath-taking had gone on in Kenya even after he had condemned these practices. He replied 'that many people respected the Queen, but nevertheless there were still gangsters in Britain. This, however, did not mean that the Queen was responsible for what they were doing.'[26]

The second side of this 'Euro-African' version of Mau Mau is the attempt to picture the whole movement as a phenomenon of only secondary importance, a side-line or an intermezzo in Kenya's history that did not really influence the course of Kenya politics before Independence. This theme, of course, is often even more implicit than the first one, because in order to propagate this view, it is sometimes quite sufficient not to mention Mau Mau at all. This happened, for example, in the special Independence issue of the *Daily Nation* (December 11, 1963) in which not a word was said on it.[27] This was certainly not because of lack of space, the issue having 64 pages, but very probably the result of a deliberate political decision, a suspicion reinforced by the tenor of Mr. Kenyatta's official speech during the Uhuru celebration on December 12. 'All the people of Kenya', said Mr. Kenyatta, 'should remember and pay tribute to those people of all races, tribes and colours who – over the years – have made their contribution to Kenya's rich heritage: administrators, farmers, missionaries, traders and others and above all the people of Kenya themselves.'[28] Not a word was said about the Mau Mau freedom-fighters who apparently had not contributed to Kenya's heritage.

Why was this? Why did Kenyatta and other leading politicians in Kenya try to belittle the contribution of the forest-fighters and why did they continue to use, even after Independence, terms and concepts that came straight from the European mythological armory? Why did they try to play down the African myth?

It is not easy to answer these questions, partly because, up till now, not much has been written on the subject,[29] and partly because several factors may have played a role in this rather complicated process. Although I do not pretend to be able to present an exhaustive account of this whole issue, I will nevertheless try to analyze at least the main reasons which have influenced the evolution of the myth of Mau Mau just before and shortly after Independence.

National Unity: We all fought for Uhuru

When Mr. Kenyatta, in August 1961, came home after having spent almost nine years in detention, Kenya was going through a most dangerous political crisis and tensions were rife all over the country. As we have seen earlier, two nation-wide political parties had just been founded, both of them more or less tribal coalitions, and one of them openly committed to regionalism, in which it was overtly supported by the colonial rulers and by part of the European and Asian minorities in Kenya. At the grassroot level, the situation was much the same: several tribal groups coveted the ex-White Highlands that were going to be opened to African farmers and some political leaders did not refrain from invoking the spectre of civil war.[30] It is therefore no wonder that Mr. Kenyatta, right from the start, made it one of the main tasks, if not *the* main task, of his political career to promote national unity above tribal antagonism. 'My message now is unity for all the people of Kenya', he announced on the 14th of August 1961, the day of his return to his homestead in Gatundu,[31] and this theme has been developed since in almost all his speeches and in all his writings. 'The most essential need which I have constantly sought to proclaim and to fulfil in Kenya', he wrote in the foreword of *Suffering without Bitterness* (1968), 'has been that of national unity; nationhood and family-hood must and can be contrived out of our many tribes and cultures. Nationalism rooted in loyalty to Kenya must come first.'[32]

It is quite clear that the memory of Mau Mau, which, if it was not a *tribal revolt*, certainly was the *revolt of one tribe*, may eventually become a negative factor in the process of nation building. It is, indeed, possible for some of the members of the Kikuyu – Embu and Meru group to be proud of the Mau Mau revolt and to identify themselves with the movement. However, it is much more difficult for a non-Kikuyu to believe in the idea that Kenya's independence was brought about by a movement in which neither he, nor other members of his tribe, took any part. Professor Mazrui stated this problem very lucidly in his article *On Heroes and Uhuru-Worship:* 'In an essay published in 1883 on the subject of "What is a Nation?", Ernest Renan observed that one essential factor in the making of a nation is "to get one's history wrong"... Certainly in regard to building up unity in Kenya a great deal of selection is needed about what to emphasize in the history of Mau Mau.'[33]

In order 'to get Kenya's history wrong' on this point, President Kenyatta and his political associates, probably quite deliberately, launched the slogan: *We all fought for Uhuru*, which since the beginning of the sixties up till today has been one of the leading themes in Kenya politics. As President Kenyatta himself said in his speech on Kenyatta Day 1967: 'Sometimes I hear of freedom fighters described as those who brought Uhuru. But I want to emphasize that freedom could not have been brought up by one person, or by a single group of people. Freedom came (to us) through AFRICAN UNITY. It was all of us being united... We were all seeking freedom (together), and therefore it is not right to discriminate, saying that one man served to bring freedom while another man did something else.'[34]

Kenyatta had to say this chiefly for political reasons, and especially because the existence of a people or group that fought and suffered more for Independence than anybody else is incompatible with the myth of Kenyan unity. As a matter of fact there is even some truth in Mr. Kenyatta's statement and in other statements such as the one made recently by Mr. Koinange, the Minister of State, when he objected in Parliament to a motion that 'tended to confine the freedom struggle to one particular group of people by mentioning the Mau Mau war and also to a special space of time. The Minister said the freedom struggle in Kenya has been a continuous process since the last century when people at the Coast resisted Arab colonisation there.'[35] Especially after the defeat of the armed revolt in 1956, other ethnic groups as well as political leaders of non-Kikuyu origin, like Tom Mboya and Oginga Odinga, took over the struggle for Kenya's independence and their contribution to Uhuru has been as important as was the contribution of the forest fighters.

People like Mboya and Odinga certainly were and are allowed to say that 'we all fought for Uhuru' without having to blush.

The theme, however, has also been used by people who's main contribution to Kenya's Independence was their attempt to continue unnoticed with the daily routine of life during the Emergency. I see, in fact, no other way of explaining the following statement by Mr. Mwendwa, in 1967 Minister for Power and Communications, during a parliamentary debate on a Motion asking for Government support for the ex-freedom fighters: 'The Minister said it was difficult to draw the line between those who had actually fought in the field for independence and those who had fought by continuing with the running of the country. Many of those who were detained during the Emergency period had since been rewarded... but the other class of people, such as himself who had taught in a school, and who had also been rewarded, could not be regarded as distinct from the 'freedom fighters'. Everyone, he said, had equally contributed to the independence struggle.'[36]

One cannot help but think that the process of getting Kenya's history wrong went much too far here, and one understands the anger of people like Mr. Kanja, who, during the Emergency, was condemned to death for his Mau Mau activities and who contemptuously suggested in the course of another discussion in Parliament some years later that Mr. Mwendwa 'was dancing like a Mkamba when the Mau Mau were fighting'.[37] Of course he was immediately ordered by the Speaker to withdraw his remark, which he did, but discussions of this kind clearly show how difficult it will be to try to arrive at a balanced view of Kenya's recent history, a view which would do justice to the Mau Mau freedom fighters without immediately putting the national unity of the country in danger.

Good relations with the English

National unity was not the only preoccupation of Mr. Kenyatta when he was released from detention in August 1961. The immediate economic situation did not augur well for the future either.

'European farmers, uncertain of the future', says Mr. Carey Jones, 'ceased to develop their farms and worked them to get what they could out of them in the quickest time. They ceased to plough back their profits and they sent their money abroad. The Asian community also began to send money abroad, but to Britain rather than India. The considerable normal capital outflow was enhanced while the normally much greater capital inflow, which had masked it, dried up ... As the farmers ceased farm development and exported their profits, so farm employment fell. To the growing numbers of unemployed in the towns was added rural unemployement.'[38]

The Kenya settlers, most of whom had stayed outwardly calm and unruffled during the hard days of the Emergency, had in fact been very anxious and had even become panic-stricken round about 1960, when it became clear that Kenya would become an independent country, probably under the leadership of Mr. Kenyatta, who at that time was the African most hated by the European population because almost every settler still considered him the real leader and architect of Mau Mau.

Quite naturally the spectre of Kenya becoming independent under Kenyatta provoked waves of fear and frustration. Many Europeans were afraid of vengeance and the expropriation of European property, and the 'subsequent happenings in the Congo, which provided a continuous background to events in Kenya, more than proved their fears. Kenya settlers, and others in the Colony, could not but ask what Kenya's fate would be in independence.'[39]

In his novel *Uhuru*, Robert Ruark strongly voices the panic and fears of the Kenya settlers, fears which he very probably shared himself, if one can believe the statement in the preface of his work that 'there is nothing in this book which has not happened, is not happening or will not happen in the near future'.[40] One of the central characters of his novel, a disillusioned white hunter who once fought against Mau Mau in the forests, for example, cries out: 'The Wog has got our own dear government and the whole wide world behind him now, and he doesn't want your sympathy or your help! All he wants is your land and your houses and your women! He wants your booze and your motor-cars and your fine clothes and most of all, he wants to be a bwana and shout "Boy!" at the top of his lungs. And you benevolent old-world niggerloving bwanas will be driven into the sea or legislated out of your lands and the country will chew at itself until it's in such a foul mess not even the bloody Russians 'll want it.'[41]

It is against these visions of doom current among the European settlers that much of what Kenyatta did and said in 1961–63 must be seen. Of course, theoretically he could have played on the fears of the settlers by creating a situation of panic and chaos in which they would have preferred leaving the country on their own initiative, thereby leaving the White Highlands free for the African masses. However, this would have created even greater problems than those which befell Guinea's Sekou Touré when he decided in 1958 to go it alone and to waive the economic assistance of France. The troubles would have been immediate, while the benefits of such a decision would only be felt some decades later, that is, if the country had survived al all.

Anyway, Kenyatta, who has always been a moderate, and a political, not an economic nationalist, probably never even considered this possibility. He thus had, right from the start, to try and win back the settlers and to stop the European exodus. This he did and with much success in a brilliant campaign that lasted for two years. On August 25, 1961, only a few days after his coming home to Gatundu, he already declared that: 'The Government of an independent Kenya will not be a gangster Government. Those who have been panicky about their property – whether land or buildings or houses – can now rest assured that the future African Government, the Kenya Government, will not deprive them of their property or rights of ownership.'[42]

The culminating point in this campaign came in 1963. During a meeting in Nakuru, in the heart of the ex-White Highlands, in August of that year, Mr. Kenyatta declared to some hundreds of European farmers and their wives: 'We want you to stay and to farm well in this country: that is the policy of this Government... What the Government needs is experience, and I don't care where it comes from. I will take it with both hands... Continue to farm your land well, and you will get all the encouragement and protection of the Government... We can all work together harmoniously to make this country great, and to show other countries in the world that different racial groups can live and work together.'[43]

'At the end', comments Mr. Kenyatta's anonymous editor, 'this European concourse all rose up to their feet, joining him in cries of HARAMBEE! Lord Delamere called this a unique and historic occasion.'[44]

However, in order to reach this goal, Mr. Kenyatta was forced to do two things which were to have a profound influence on the relations between the Kenya Government and the Mau Mau freedom fighters on the one hand and on the image of the Mau Mau revolt as it exists in Kenya today on the other hand. First of all, he had to play down Mau Mau as much as possible because most of the fears of the settlers were intimately connected with the horrible memories of the Emergency days. What the Europeans were afraid of was not so much an independent Kenya, but a Mau Mau dominated Kenya. It is in this light that we should view statements that Mau Mau is a disease best forgotten as quickly as possible. Mau Mau had to be forgotten because the memory of the revolt would jar relations not only with the Kenya settlers but also with the British Government.

Secondly, Mr. Kenyatta was forced to 'betray' one of the two main ideas the whole Mau Mau movement had stood for. The Mau Mau armed forces were known as the Land Freedom Army. Freedom was there, or within reach in 1962–63, but by 'land' the freedom fighters meant that the European farmers must leave the country and that their land be freely distributed to landless Africans. The settlers had other ideas and Kenyatta's solution to the problem was not a compromise but a complete surrender to the Europeans. Of course, some parts of the ex-White Highlands were declared African settlement areas and some European farmers were forced to leave. However, their farms were purchased with money granted by or given as loans by the British Government, and at prices which, according to one author were 'one of the most generous compensations for political losses of land ownership known in economic history'.[45] African farmers, in their turn, had to pay for the land on the settlement schemes, even if they were ex-forest-fighters.

Even today this is still a hot issue in Kenya politics and political leaders close to the Mau Mau ideology regularly complain that: 'We were struggling to regain our own lands which were stolen by the British colonial government. We were not fighting for the right to buy our own land'.[46] More recently Mr. Kanja struck the same note when he told the National Assembly that 'the African in Kenya is acting like a "toothless bulldog" by continuing to bargain for land from the "enemy" when he specifically waged a bloody freedom war for it.'[47] The Kenya Government, however, has invariably stuck to its 'willing buyer – willing seller' principle, and at the end of 1971 there were still between 400 and 450 expatriate farmers in Kenya owning nearly one million hectares of land.[48]

Forgive and forget: The Loyalists

It is interesting that most of the administrative records referring to the Emergency period have been destroyed or removed and cannot be consulted any more. It is even more interesting that they may have been destroyed partly by the colonial civil servants before independence and partly *by incoming Kenya administrators afterwards.*[49] It is sometimes even said that President Kenyatta personally ordered this destruction, an eventuality which cannot be completely ruled out. Such an order, in fact, coincides very well with the slogan of 'forgive and forget' which Mr. Kenyatta launched in the early sixties when he took over the reins of power, and which he himself formulated later on in the following words: 'In a speech.... on

56

1. A historical encounter: Field-marshal Mwariama, after leaving the Mount Kenya Forest, pays a visit to Mr. Kenyatta, then Prime Minister, on December 7, 1963.
(All photo's by kind permission of the Nation Newspapers, Nairobi).

2. President Kenyatta laying the foundation stone of the Dedan Kimathi Memorial Library in Nyeri District, March 28, 1971. In his speech much honour was bestowed on the freedom fighters.

3. 'A living Memorial to Dedan Kimathi'. Fundraising campaign for the proposed Kimathi Institute of Technology, August 1971. Chairing the meeting is Mr. Mwai Kibaki, Minister of Finance and Economic Development.

4. 'Mau Mau is still alive'. Members of the Nakuru District Ex-Freedom Fighters Organisation dressed as Mau Mau warriors during a solidarity meeting for President Kenyatta in November 1971.

Kenyatta Day in 1964, I proclaimed to the people, and to all friends of this country, that the foundations of our future must lie in the theme: Forgive and forget. There is no point then, and there is still less purpose today, in dwelling on the past, in stoking fires of revenge or animosity; in looking back on scenes of anguish. Uhuru for Kenya had to be joyful, not sombre; vigorous rather than brooding.'[50]

The first ones who qualified for forgiveness were of course the Europeans, especially the Kenya settlers who, up till about 1960, so stubbornly resisted all attempts towards African emancipation. The point has certainly not been lost upon them as is clear from the words of praise Mr. MacDonald, the last Governor of Kenya, had for President Kenyatta's magnanimity in his foreword to *Harambee*, a collection of the President's speeches.[51] A second category destined for forgiveness were the Home Guards and all those amongst the Kikuyu and other ethnic groups who, as so-called Loyalists, had collaborated with the colonial Government during the Emergency. They were quite an important group numerically,[52] and as they were on the winning side during the period 1952–1961 they held many important positions.

Mr. Kenyatta's decision not to change anything in this situation occurred very early in the second part of his political career. When, in March 1961, one of his political friends mentioned the problem of the factions in Central Province, of those who were in the forest and in detention camps on the one hand, and the loyalists on the other, factions which both claimed to have his support, Kenyatta answered: 'I am not for those who have been in the forest or detention camps, I am for the African people. All of them'[53]. And in his New Year's message for 1971 he still felt obliged to come back to this point by saying that 'to forgive collaborators was a way of healing such elements like mistrust and division for the well-being of the nation'.[54]

The ex-freedom fighters might have been willing to 'forgive' their enemies, although even this must have been very difficult for many of them. They or at least some of them were certainly not willing to *forget*, and they have not hesitated to say so. Some did it ironically, like Mr. Kanja in a recent declaration in Parliament where he said that 'everything has a start, and you cannot forget your birthday. You still celebrate your birthday.'[55] Others did it in a more lyrical and dramatic way like James Ngugi, Kenya's first and still leading novelist, who, through an ex-detainee, asks: 'How forget the past? How forget my yesterday of humiliation, my yesterday of whip-lashes on my back, my yesterday of sweat for another's stomach, my yesterday of shame, degradation, exploitation! For me there is no tomorrow without yesterday and I will so fan my wounds alive that they will hurt hour by hour, a watchdog for a second betrayal by my rich brothers... No. The fire of my anger, my shame is my legacy to my children.'[56]

Whatever one's position is in this debate, it is clear that Kenyatta's policy of national reconciliation and of forgiving the Home Guards induced him to play down the role of Mau Mau in the freedom struggle and even occasionally to pour scorn upon it as something bad or primitive. If Home Guards and Loyalists are to recognize themselves in the mirror of Kenya's history, then this mirror should not only or exclusively, reflect Mau Mau heroes.

Kenyatta's own role
It is a characteristic feature of Kenya politics today that each year on October 20, the day of the Emergency declaration, the country celebrates *Kenyatta Day* and not *Mau Mau Day* or something like it. This means that President Kenyatta is trying to create his own myth in Kenya historiography or has allowed others to do so, which certainly was bound to have an effect on the way the myth of Mau Mau has been handled on the official level. In fact, the two myths are in a way incompatible. If one wants to boost the role of Mr. Kenyatta in the history of the Independence struggle, one has to emphasize the period up till October 1952, when he was arrested, and again the period starting in the summer of 1961 when he was released from detention. These were the days that Kenyatta dominated the scene. However, from October 1952 until 1961, Kenyatta was tucked away in jail and did not play a direct or active role in the historical events of the day. Seen from his own point of view, then, this period should best be treated as a sort of 'historical vacuum', an interlude during which nothing of real importance happened.

The only way out would have been to proclaim *urbi et orbi* that Kenyatta had always been and still was the real leader of Mau Mau, which at the same time would have meant a complete change from his line of defence adopted during the Kapenguria trial in 1953. Kenyatta never seriously tried to do this, and in his book *Suffering without Bitterness* a whole chapter is devoted to the Kapenguria trial in which he denies in vehement terms – the same that were used in 1953 – that he had anything to do with Mau Mau or that he advocated in any way a policy of violence or 'lawlessness': 'Those who built up an organization of unbridled violence in Kenya were never the political associates or executive colleagues of Kenyatta', as he says in his own words.[57] So harsh and resentful are the words he uses to express his antipathy and aversion for the Mau Mau struggle, especially when one recollects the generosity he showed to the ex-colonial rulers, that one even wonders whether Kenyatta, unconsciously, does not lay the blame for his nine years in detention at the door of the Mau Mau leaders, who in a way provoked the State of Emergency, rather than with the colonial administrators.

In any case the incompatibility of the myth of Mau Mau and the myth of Kenyatta as the Father of the Nation does throw some light on the ambivalent feelings many Kenyans have today about the Mau Mau period. If Kenyatta is *the* leader who has led Kenya towards Independence, then Mau Mau, of which Kenyatta never was a leader according to his own consistent testimony, cannot have played such an important role in the history of East Africa. And if Kenyatta can, in 1968, reprint his declaration at Kapenguria in an unchanged form that Mau Mau was a bad thing that had 'spoiled the country'[58], then one wonders how the revolt can ever become a positive myth in Kenya.[59]

The forest fighters' menace

The four factors which have been mentioned so far (national unity, good relations with the British, reconciliation between the Mau Mau fighters and the Loyalists, and Kenyatta's own place in history) are probably the most important causes at the root of the 'Euro-African', official myth of Mau Mau. Other factors probably also played a role – though a minor one – and will only receive scant attention here.

The menace the surviving forest-fighters army was supposed to be at the end of 1963, on the dawn of Independence, is the first of these factors. The British Army and the other armed forces in Kenya had in fact left the forest fighters in peace after the major defeat of

59

the Mau Mau armies, a defeat the Mount Kenya forces suffered in 1954 and the Aberdare groups in 1955–56. The Mount Kenya area, however, was never really cleared and at the end of 1963, it became suddenly evident that hundreds, which later turned out to be thousands, of more or less 'forgotten' freedom fighters still lived on the Mountain especially near Meru District. In December 1963 the Kenya Government ordered them to 'surrender' (a revealing term in itself!) and negotiations between Government emissaries and the last Mau Mau field-marshals started. They subsequently left the forest with their men, but especially in the beginning relations between both parties were rather strained. The forest-fighters behaved as if they were above the law and threatened violent action if they did not get their way. At the same time the Government was not inclined to give in and satisfy the demands of the field-marshals.

Finally, some of them, disgruntled and dissatisfied with the way things had developed since Uhuru, again withdrew to the forest where, ironically, they were crushed by the armed forces of Independent Kenya in 1964–65.[60]

It is impossible to say in how far the dissident freedom fighters were ever a real menace to order and stability in the country, but for some time it was feared that they might join hands with the *shifta* from the North Eastern Province, and some people (including Kenyatta?) may have been sincerely afraid that the forest fighters would form a sort of 'alternative' government. The following news item from *Africa Research Bulletin*, Vol I(1), January 1964, leads one to think that such fears were not altogether without foundation: '"Marshal" Baimunge, a forest fighter from the Mount Kenya forest is reported to have told a meeting... that people should respect him as they did the Prime Minister. The Information Officer of Meru County Council said that he had forced men and women to remove their hats or head coverings.' These fears may have reinforced the campaign to 'play down the Mau Mau' which was already going on for some time.

Uhuru na Kazi

The myth of Mau Mau also indirectly clashed with another slogan launched by Mr. Kenyatta in the early 1960s: *Uhuru na Kazi* or Independence and Work. It is indeed a fact that too many Africans in different parts of the continent thought – consciously or not – that with Independence paradise would be established on earth. The idea that independence would first and foremost mean hard work and abnegation has been very slow in taking form. Kenyatta, and with him other African leaders like Mr. Nyerere from Tanzania, was thus quite well inspired when he insisted right from the start upon the necessity for everybody to work hard and build up the new nation.

In itself this has nothing to do with Mau Mau, and there would never have been any connection at all, had not some freedom fighters insistently and loudly asked for 'free things' i.e. substantial government support in the fields of settlement, housing and education. We will come back to this subject in chapter four of this book, when the specific claims of the freedom fighters will be considered in detail, but it is of course quite clear that too much emphasis on 'free things' went against Kenyatta's policy of hard work and self-help activities, while it must also be said that the Kenya economy would never have been able to support a class of 'prebendaries' living entirely or partly on public funds.

By playing down the role of Mau Mau in the struggle for Independence it was possible to check the sometimes exaggerated demands of the forest fighters.

The skeleton in the cupboard

There are many indications to prove that not only all the Europeans in Kenya and outside but also quite a few Africans fell for the European myth of Mau Mau. Let me just quote two examples. The first is Mr. M.A. Amalemba who, in the beginning of 1960, expressed his feelings on Mau Mau in the following words: 'Ce fut en réalité un mouvement de révolte primitif et régressif destiné à renverser le Gouvernement légal et régulier de ce pays... Une révolte... dont les membres étaient prêts à commettre les actes les plus honteux et les plus bestiaux, impossible à décrire en public... une telle révolte ne peut être classée dans les mouvements nationaux.'[61] And he concluded by thanking the British Government for its financial contribution to the expenditures caused by the Emergency.[62]

The second example is the late Harry Thuku, who once had been an outstanding Kenya nationalist. He too condemned Mau Mau outrightly, for example in a letter to one of his friends in England dated December 21, 1954, in which he says: 'You may be interested to hear the state of affairs in Kikuyu country today. The evils of devil have for three years tried to shake the good work done by the churches. But I am glad to say that Christians of all denominations stood firm with their faith in Christ.'[63]

These quotations clearly prove that many Kenya Africans imbibed a part or the whole of the European myth of Mau Mau, a trend which was not completely reversed after Independence. As some of Kenyatta's co-detainees during the Emergency reveal in their introduction to 'Mau Mau from Within', even the behaviour of many ex-freedom fighters who were members of the Land Freedom Army, tends to be deliberately self-effacing and diffident today, an attitude arising out of a sense of guilt built up during the years of 'brain washing' in the 'rehabilitation' camps of the colonial days.[64] It is probably an exaggeration to say, as C.R. Larson does, that 'for independent Kenya, Mau Mauism has become something akin to Nazism in the Germany of past-World War II',[65] but it is certainly true that for those Kenyans who have 'interiorized' the European version of the Emergency events, Mau Mau must in a certain sense be 'the skeleton in Kenya's cupboard'. These feelings may very well have been the basis of the 'Euro-African' myth of Mau Mau elaborated by Kenyatta and his collaborators. In any case they certainly helped to propagate this version of the Emergency.

C. The Myth of Mau Mau today

Roughly speaking one may say that the 'Euro-African' myth of Mau Mau was not completely successful in entrenching itself and we are probably going through a sort of intermediary phase today. First of all, Mau Mau is far from forgotten, and it seems that we are even witnessing a sort of Mau Mau 'revival' in public life. Especially in 1971, news on Mau Mau or related topics on several occasions has reached the front-page news both in the *Daily Nation*, and in its Swahili counterpart *Taifa Leo*. A Kenya monthly review, the *Kenya Mirror*, even came out with a Mau Mau special at the end of 1971.[66] From discussions with journalists one gets the impression that the Kenya public is genuinely interested in everything that is connected with Mau Mau, an observation endorsed by leading Nairobi publishers; books on Mau Mau generally sell well, even if they are badly written. General China's '*Mau Mau*' *General* has already been reprinted, and it is felt in the publishing world in Nairobi, that several of the Memoirs of ex-Mau Mau freedom fighters published during the last two years, will also sell very well.

Kenyatta's attitude

It seems also that President Kenyatta himself changed his mind on Mau Mau. Several of his recent speeches, in fact, indicate that he has at least abandoned in part the 'Euro-African' myth he seemed to favour during the period 1961–64. First of all, Mr. Kenyatta no longer ignores the Mau Mau revolt, as he did in his Independence Speech in 1963, but openly recognizes the role of the movement in the struggle for Independence. 'Brothers', he said for example in his speech on Kenyatta Day 1967, 'you all know that this day is one of great inspiration. It is very important, because without (the events sparked off by) October 20, 1952, we would still be chained and handcuffed by the colonialists. Those who do not realise this are foolish men.'[67] It would now be impossible in Kenya to say, as one of the Members of Parliament did in November 1964, that 'I believe we obtained our independence in a very nice way at the instigation of the British Government but not through fighting in the forest'.[68]

Kenyatta's watchword today is quite clear: 'We snatched our Uhuru from the colonialists'.

Here we have a clear attempt to accommodate Mau Mau again into Kenya's history. A similar attempt was made during the summer of 1971 when Mr. Kenyatta, during his working holiday in the Coast Province, ordered the name of the town of Galole to be changed to Hola, as the place was called where in 1960 11 Mau Mau detainees died after having been severely beaten and maltreated by their guards. The colonial rulers quickly changed the name of the camp, but in 1971 Hola was thus brought back on the map again in order 'to tie up with Kenya's history'.

Mr. Kenyatta went further than he had ever gone before in paying tribute to the Mau Mau freedom fighters in March 1971, when he laid the foundation stone of the Kimathi Memorial Library at a school six miles west of Nyeri township and situated about 800 yards from the spot where Dedan Kimathi, the general leader of the Mau Mau armies, was shot and arrested by the Colonial police in 1956. 'Speaking in a grave tone Mzee told the gathering that there was nothing the living generation could do to repay the efforts of the people who died or were deformed or impoverished by the consequences of the struggle for Uhuru. Mzee stressed that many people were killed, and others were still alive – 'but we could not thank them enough for the job they accomplished...' ...The President noted that the struggle for Uhuru deprived Kenya of great national heroes – 'like Dedan Kimathi and Stanley Mathenge and many others.'[69] According to local eyewitnesses President Kenyatta also ordered that the exact place where Kimathi was captured should be clearly marked. In September 1971, when I visited the region, this had indeed been done, even if only in a very simple way.

How is Kenyatta's change of heart to be explained? While there may be several reasons that still actually completely escape us, two factors may be mentioned at least, which flow from the actual political situation in Kenya and in the world in general.

The first one is only a supposition for which I have no proof at all and which may even be completely off the mark. It is often said in Kenya that Kenyatta has bestowed too much favours on his home district Kiambu since he came into power, and that for this reason not even all the Kikuyu are now behind him. The Fort Hall and Nyeri Kikuyu seem to show signs of dissatisfaction and frustration, a fact which narrows Mr. Kenyatta's political basis very much... maybe too much even. Now it can roughly speaking be said, that most of the Mau Mau guerilla activities have been the work of the people of Nyeri and Fort Hall, while Kiambu district remained 'neutral' and stood aside during the armed struggle. It is then possible to argue that Kenyatta's more favourable statements on Mau Mau during the last few years form part of an attempt to arrive at a better equilibrium of the political forces in Kikuyu-land in order not to alienate completely Nyeri and Fort Hall District.

A second reason is probably that the spectre of Mau Mau as a form of danger has diminished as the years go by. We have seen that there were at least four main reasons why Mau Mau had to be played down by the Kenyatta Government around Independence. One of them, the European nightmare of a Mau Mau dominated 'gangster' administration, was no longer in existence at the beginning of 1971 after seven years of 'moderate' politics by the incumbent Kenya elite. The relationship with the Kenya settlers has been excellent, almost cloudless, since Kenyatta's historical speech in Nakuru, and I do not know of a single case where European property was expropriated without due compensation. The relations with the ex-colonial rulers are also good. Kenya is internationally, at least in the Western world, known as a moderate, stable and well-administered country, a 'sound bet for trade and investment', as J. Young recently said in a *Times Supplement* on Kenya.[70] Today the simple fact of laying the foundation stone of a Kimathi Memorial Library and praising the forest fighters is not enough to revive the fears that once existed in European hearts.

A loyalist offensive?

What about the other factors that were at the root of the 'Euro-African' myth of Mau Mau and which may still prevent the rehabilitation of the revolt in public life?

As far as Kenyatta's own position is concerned we can be rather brief. Apparently, he is less anxious today that the myth of Mau Mau might eclipse his own legend as a national hero. In any case, his dominating position in Kenya politics is temporary. After his death, it will probably be quite easy to reconcile, in one way or another, the two myths or let them exist side by side in harmony by skilfully dissimulating eventual inconsistencies. Dogmas, and even historical dogmas do not necessarily have to be mutually compatible to be believed in.

The ex-Loyalists and their descendants might pose a more difficult problem. Up till now, when papers like the *Kenya Mirror* carry enthusiastic articles on the heroic exploits of Dedan Kimathi and the other freedom fighters, the reactions are mostly one-sided. Letters to the editor, at least those that have been published, are almost invariably favourably disposed to Mau Mau and often go even further in their praise of Mau Mau than the articles in question. Loyalists and anti-Mau Mau people are apparently lying low at the moment, although it is clear that quite a few people in Kenya and even in Kikuyu-land do not at all like the sort of Mau Mau 'revival' we are witnessing today.

This, however, might change in the near future, if one has to believe the following news item that appeared in the *Daily Nation* of August 27, 1971: 'Although the political and intellectual climate of the day is not congenial to their views, Loyalists during the Mau Mau struggle should be encouraged to write their views, Professor Bethwell A. Ogot, Deputy Vice-Chancellor and Professor of History of the University of Nairobi, said in a paper he presented at the Historical Association of Kenya in Nairobi yesterday. Giving reasons for encouraging the loyalists to write their memories, he said 'history is a science and cannot be based on popular myths'.[71] Professor Ogot is probably not the only one who is hoping for such a 'loyalist offensive' which, although announced as a purely scientific and academic affair, will undoubtedly have political overtones.

Until now, nothing has been published from the loyalists' side, if one excludes the autobiography of Harry Thuku who practically does not mention Mau Mau, except for a few pages at the end of his book. Other books, however, may appear during the next few years[72] in which case, a confrontation between the two sides – Loyalists and ex-Freedom Fighters – will be inevitable. It is difficult to predict what will happen in that event because much will depend on the political situation of the day. In the long run, however, when the Loyalists will have died out, some kind of compromise between the two myths will probably be reached in a way that would do justice to Mau Mau, without tarnishing overmuch the reputation of the Loyalists.

Mau Mau and the other tribes

The greatest obstacle on the way to a Mau Mau rehabilitation will probably be the set of attitudes towards the revolt still prevalent among non-Kikuyu groups. We have already had occasion to quote Mr. Amalemba's opinion on Mau Mau, and it is very probable that many non-Kikuyu in Kenya still think on the same lines. I will always remember how a Luhya, when I informed him of a Cabinet Minister's suggestion that roads should be named after Mau Mau, spontaneously exclaimed: 'My God, I wouldn't like to walk on such a road'[73]

Even for non-Kikuyu who are favourably disposed towards the revolt, it may prove very hard to integrate Mau Mau in a genuinely harmonious way into their vision of Kenya history. Oginga Odinga is a good example of this category. All through his book he leaves no doubt at all that he values Mau Mau as a positive factor in the struggle for Independence and he even endorses the principal theses that are part of the African myth of the revolt: For him, Mau Mau 'represented an all-Kenya nationalism with advanced and clearly stated political aims,'[74] and the 'Emergency was a time of revolutionary war'.[75]

However, when he discusses his own role during the Emergency, and especially when he tries to explain why he was not arrested during this period, some problems crop up. 'The government was intent on rounding up every possible KAU supporter in Nyanza', Odinga says, 'but it was conscious that if it did not tread warily, the Luo might be provoked, as the result of the arrest of their most prominent leaders, into direct involvement on the side of the freedom fighters. I think it was to this need to step warily that I owe the fact that I was not detained, though there were times when I thought I had narrowly missed being arrested... My arrest, the government must have known, might have meant the incitement to rebellion of Luo: it would have been stupid tactics to open a new front of struggle in Nyanza.'[76]

In a way then, Odinga could sit through the Emergency without difficulties because neither he nor his people were really involved in the revolt, a factor which must make it very difficult for him and his ilk to identify themselves completely with Mau Mau. The whole problem of Mau Mau and the other tribes is very nicely summed up in a letter to the editor written in reaction to an article in the *Kenya Mirror* of August 1971:

'I was... disappointed to note in your article on Mau Mau Legend that *only the Kikuyu people have been credited with the forest fighters.* I agree that our Kikuyu brothers and sisters suffered a great deal during the Emergency but you should not forget the contribution of the Luo and Wakamba leaders... Prominent Luo leaders like Tom Mboya and Oginga Odinga kept the freedom fight going. Was it not Odinga who gave Kenya the slogan of *Uhuru na Kenyatta?* Was it not Tom Mboya who organised the workers of Kenya to struggle against the colonialists? I do very much hope that when the Kenya Mirror writes about the Mau Mau Movement in the future these great contributions of all Kenyans will be duly acknowledged.'[77]

Unhappily however, although Tom Mboya and Oginga Odinga were responsible for many very laudable actions in the Kenya Independence struggle, the only thing they cannot claim is that they took part in the forest fight, i.e. in the Mau Mau revolt. It is true, as J. M. Kariuki stated, that members of other tribes took part in the Mau Mau movement and maybe even in the forest fight, but *by the fact of doing so they ceased to be representative of their groups.* They were isolated, uprooted and detribalized individuals, not real members of their tribe. As we said, this hard fact will probably be the greatest stumbling-block for those who are trying to transform the legend of Mau Mau into a national myth.

Mau Mau as a tribal legend

One gets the impression that Kenya's political leaders, either unintentionally or with the purpose of overcoming this dilemma, actually pursue a double-edged policy concerning the myth of Mau Mau: on the one hand, they do not seem to exert themselves to build up a national historical myth around Mau Mau but on the other, they are apparently not opposed to the eventuality of Mau Mau becoming a sort of tribal legend.

It is in this way that I am inclined to interpret Dr. Kiano's answer to a question in Parliament why no roads in the Republic were named after the freedom war, or why the Government refrained from selecting a suitable street in Nairobi and name it 'Mau Mau Road'. According to the *Daily Nation* the Minister for Local Government 'informed the Member that it was the responsibility of local authorities to select names of their respective streets and seek approval of his Ministry. One street in Nairobi was named after Dedan Kimathi, who was a leading figure in the Mau Mau movement. He was sure that many local councils would take the suggestion and flood his office with applications to name roads after Mau Mau.'[78] It would indeed seem a sound measure in this domain to give the green light to local communities favourably disposed towards Mau Mau without forcing non-Kikuyu groups to feign interest in a movement with which they can scarcely be expected to identify themselves.

Indications of this Government policy of 'localization' of the Mau Mau legend can also be found, in my opinion, in the apparently contradictory way the very controversial issue of Kimathi's

68

grave and eventual memorial has been handled recently by the Kenya Government. The issue has been raised regularly in Parliament and in the Press, the first time even before Independence when Mr. Francis Ngunjiri, the author of an unpublished play on the life of Dedan Kimathi, in a sort of open letter to the Nyeri Members of the National Assembly, suggested 'that a statue of Dedan Kimathi should be erected in Delamere Avenue, in place of the Delamere statue which was removed recently'.[79]

Since the end of 1968 this affair has been brought up in Parliament at least three times, and it is interesting to go into this in some detail in order to analyze the fluctuations and meandering of Government policy on this point. The first time the issue was raised was in December 1968 when the debate was reported in the *East African Standard* in the following terms:

'A Minister of State in the President's Office, Mr. Koinange told Parliament... that the late Mau Mau 'Field Marshal' Dedan Kimathi... was buried at Kamiti Prison and that his grave was fenced. The Government appreciated that he was a hero in the struggle for freedom and welcomed the suggestion of building a monument to him in the future. Plans were afoot to see how a better grave could be prepared... He declined to comment on a suggestion that Kimathi's grave and monument should be constructed along Kenyatta Avenue, adding that the grave would be put in a better place.'[80]

Exactly five years after the Independence celebrations, the position of the Kenya Government seemed quite clear and it looked as if the building of a monument and the preparation of a proper grave was then only a question of time. However, in November 1969, the Government had quite evidently fallen back to a more ambiguous position, according to a short paragraph in the Parliamentary column of the *Daily Nation:* 'An Assistant Minister for Finance, Mr. S. M. Balala, told the House that the Government does recognise the excellent work done by the late freedom fighters, namely Mr. Dedan Kimathi, Mr. Stanley Mathenge and 'General' Kubukubu, and others who fought for Kenya's independence. Replying to Mr. Kamwithi Munyi (Embu East), he said there were no plans at the present to build monuments in those people's memory but this did not rule out the possibility of such monuments being built in future.'[81] One definitely gets the impression here that the Government was employing delaying tactics and that Mr. Munyi was fobbed off with fair promises.

In September 1971 the Government's position apparently had become even more negative. At that time the same Mr. Munyi, now an Assistant Minister in the Office of the President, indeed rejected on behalf of the Government, a demand of some Members of Parliament 'that the body of the late hero and leader of the freedom movement in Kenya, Dedan Kimathi, be removed from Kamiti and be reburied ceremoniously in his home district, Nyeri'.[82]

Here, for the first time, the demand met with a plain rebuff, but it is interesting to analyse the reasons for this refusal put forward by the Government spokesman. To begin with, he hinted 'that it is likely that a technical problem would arise if the request was met because it is likely that the late Dedan Kimathi was buried in a common grave amongst other freedom fighters. It might be a problem to identify his body.'[83] More interesting, however, for an understanding of the subtleties of the official standpoint of the Kenya Government on Mau Mau, are the following statements: 'Mrs. Grace Onyango (Kisumu Town) asked if the Minister... could find about the graves of heroes of other tribes like the late Mr. Ofafa (Mr. Ofafa is believed to have been murdered by Mau Mau as a Loyalist and not by the then administration). Mr. Munyi said to single freedom fighters out for a ceremonial burial would not be consistent with the spirit of building a united nation and it would in addition be a waste of public funds and time to locate graves and exhume their remains.'[84]

But Mr. Munyi concluded his remarks by reminding his audience 'that in appreciation of the good work done by these men the Government had allowed many monuments to be erected as a remembrance of their services to Kenya'.[85]

First of all this debate demonstrates the actual impossibility for any Government in Kenya to give too much importance to the Mau Mau fighters and to transform their struggle into a national myth: members of other tribes would certainly complain about the waste of public funds. Mrs. Onyango's query is characteristic of their quick and irritated reactions. The case of the late Mr. Ofafa is particularly interesting, because even Oginga Odinga, while claiming all through his book to be a staunch supporter of the ex-freedom fighters, actively contributed to the fundraising campaigns launched in order to build a Ofafa Memorial Hall in Kisumu.[86] Such divided loyalties – and in most cases they are not even divided – make a national policy on Mau Mau almost impossible.

At the same time, however, the Government's spokesman gave plainly to understand that the authorities are in no way opposed to local initiatives to honour Mau Mau and the freedom fighters as long as they are locally financed. There are several instances to substantiate the hypothesis that Mr. Kenyatta and his Government have indeed given the green light to eventual efforts to build up Mau Mau into a positive myth on the Central Provincial level and eventually in other Kikuyu-dominated areas. Very interesting is the following news item that appeared in the *Daily Nation* of December 21, 1971: 'A suitable monument for "Uhuru heroes" is at present being discussed between the Nairobi City Council and the Ministry of Local Government for Kenya's capital city. In addition to an appropriate monument in memory of Dedan Kimathi, in place of the King George V Memorial Foundation near the National Assembly, another monument is also planned for Harry Thuku.'[87]

Here the Government is giving, what it refused to give only a few months before, although there is an interesting attempt to counter-balance the homage to Kimathi by proposing to honour the loyalist Harry Thuku at the same time.[88] Apparently then, proposals to build memorials for Mau Mau heroes are accepted *as long as the initiative comes from the local authorities and as long as central Government funds are not directly involved.*

This can also be deduced from the case of the proposed Kimathi Institute of Technology, a Nyeri district self-help project with an estimated cost of £ 500.000 which was first mentioned in the Kenya newspapers on September 2, 1971. This Institute which is explicitly meant by its sponsors as 'a living memorial for Dedan Kimathi the freedom fighter',[89] has received much publicity in the press right from the start and is sponsored by top-level politicians and civil servants such as Mr. Mwai Kibaki, the Minister for Finance and Economic Planning, and Mr. Duncan Ndegwa, the Governor of the Central Bank of Kenya. President Kenyatta even accepted to be the Patron of the Institute. The association of this project, in which the prestige of the whole of Nyeri district is clearly at stake, with the memory of Dedan Kimathi became even clearer in January 1972, when Mr. Kibaki disclosed that, in order to raise funds for the Institute, badges would be sold bearing the picture of Dedan Kimathi. According to the Minister 500.000 badges were initially produced to be sold at 2/– a piece. The picture selected was the last of Kimathi after he had been captured. 'It is the last image of a man who died struggling for Kenya's independence', Mr. Kibaki declared at a pressmeeting.[90]

Something rather similar is happening in Hola District, where it was announced recently that a fund-raising campaign was to be inaugurated in order to build a monument in remembrance of the 11 Mau Mau detainees who were beaten to death in Hola camp in March 1959. Again, a local initiative with local funds, although the principal sponsor of the project, Mr. J. Z. Kase, Assistant Minister for Information and Broadcasting, also claimed that his group would receive Government help.[91]

On first sight the Government policy on Mau Mau memorials, then, would appear to be rather vacillating and contradictory, but a more thorough-going analysis suggests that there might be 'some method in this madness', in the sense that the Kenya Government seems to distinguish sharply between the national level, where it has to steer a middle course between conflicting interests and myths, and the local level where people are more or less left free to follow their inclinations in honouring the freedom fighters.

D. Mau Mau in historiography

There can be no doubt that many of the Mau Mau forest fighters, especially during the last years of the armed struggle, when they were already on the loosing end, were very much pre-occupied by the place coming generations would assign to their struggle in Kenya's history. Karari Njama, for example, expressed the hope that the 'Kenya Young Stars Association', an association of the Aberdare forest fighters founded by Dedan Kimathi, would be recorded in history as the 'Light of Kenya During Kenya's Dark Ages,'[92] and his co-author D. L. Barnett, when commenting on the philosophy and the mental world of the forest fighters, insists on their 'almost urgent desire that the exploits, struggles and sacrifices of the forest revolutionaries not be forgotten or undervalued by future Kikuyu and Kenya African generations'.[93] The same preoccupations are ascribed to them by G. Wachira, in his novel *Ordeal in the Forest*, in a passage where one of the characters expresses his wish that the Mau Mau struggle be 'emblazoned in the history books'.[94]

Given this preoccupation, we will devote a special section of this chapter to the image of Mau Mau in historiography, although it is of course not always easy to separate the myth of Mau Mau in historiography from that of Mau Mau in public life.

A reluctant university

During the Annual Conference of the Historical Association of Kenya, held in 1971, O.W. Furley of Makerere College delivered a paper on the 'Historiography of Mau Mau' which received much attention in the Kenya Press and particularly in the *Daily Nation*. Mr. Furley's conclusions, for example, were quoted extensively in the *Daily Nation* of August 26, 1971:

'Many Governments after a major war is over, have sponsored and financed an "official history" of the war, where government resources have enabled research "in depth" to be carried out, so that a "definitive" history may emerge. One feels independent Kenya, looking back on the struggle, could very legitimately launch such a programme and raise the historiography of Mau Mau to a new level of knowledge and enlightenment.'

The same article also mentioned Mr. Furley's plea for ' a massive pursuit of oral histories of Mau Mau before memories grow dim'.[95] A few days later, in an editorial, entitled 'Analysing Mau Mau', the *Daily Nation* came back to this question, concluding that it is 'very imperative to dig deeper into the antecedents and the aftermath of the struggle'.[96]

Is there any chance that Mr. Furley's pleas will fall on fertile soil? And if so, in what direction is the interpretation of Mau Mau as a historical phenomenon likely to be? Although it is by no means easy I shall attempt to answer these questions here. In fact, in talking to University professors in Nairobi and other people interested in the problem one gets the impression, that we are actually going through a period of intermission in the historiography of Mau Mau, which makes it difficult to perceive clearly the tendencies for the future.

It can be said, however, that the collection of oral histories of

73

Mau Mau, for which Mr. Furley argued, is indeed pursued with much enthusiasm by Prof. Ogot and other staff-members of the History Department of the University of Nairobi as well as by John Nottingham of the East African Publishing House. During the summer of 1971 the memoires of two forest fighters appeared almost simultaneously,[97] while several other personal documents are scheduled to appear in 1972, among which is a very important book by Bildad Kaggia who played a key role in the Mau Mau movement during the period 1950–52. As we mentioned before, Professor Ogot is also actively trying to persuade outstanding Loyalists to present their point of view of the Mau Mau period.

On the other hand, there are actually, as far as I know, no plans to take up Mr. Furley's main suggestion to prepare a sort of Government sponsored and financed 'official' history of the Mau Mau revolt. In University circles the tendency appears to be to wait first until more material on the Emergency period is available, before once more taking up the task of historical analysis. According to Professor Ogot, it will certainly take some more years before a definite comparison of the manyfold viewpoints is possible. As for the direction the interpretation of Mau Mau will take one has to consider that Kenya's leading historians are actually mostly of non-Kikuyu origin and that they seem rather reluctant to go the 'whole hog' with the African myth of Mau Mau. Mau Mau is considered by them to be a 'proto-nationalist' rather than a nationalist movement, and it is clear that Prof. Ogot at least is slightly irritated by the more excessive versions of the African myth of the revolt. By encouraging the loyalists to speak he hopes to come to a more balanced view of the Emergency which would do justice to both camps in the struggle. It is therefore quite probable that during the coming years Mau Mau will receive more attention in historiography. Still it will be played down much more than the forest-fighters once hoped in the heat of the struggle.

Mau Mau in the classroom
I have not been able to make a detailed and complete survey of all the school books used in history classes in Kenya, partly due to lack of time, but also because the Inspectorate of the Ministry of Education recommends certain history books, but does not dictate their use. History teachers thus have some degree of freedom and it

is impossible to say what books are in actual use and by whom. It is, however, possible with the help of the Lists of Books published by the Ministry and the impressions of Kenya publishers and booksellers, to get at least some idea of how Mau Mau is presented in the classroom. We may as well start this analysis by saying that the presentation of Mau Mau in history classes has always been a problem. 'I find it quite incredible,' said John Nottingham, some years ago, 'that in 1965 in Kenya one of the recommended class books for the primary school history syllabus was used as a basis for the so-called "rehabilitation" of the detainees in Kenya's Emergency Camps.'[98]

As far as I know this specific book is not used anymore today. Yet one still finds on the Official History Book Lists for the first four forms of secondary schools[99] several books with a very negative and openly colonialistic image of the Mau Mau movement. Although it only devotes a few pages to the decolonisation process and says nothing about Mau Mau, E. Loftus' *A visual History of East Africa* is a good example of this category of books. The following passages are indeed quite revealing:

'Progress towards full self-government [in East Africa] was under the guidance of, and with financial aid from, the country which is best able to lead towards that desirable end. For Britian has probably done more than any other country to preserve the "freedoms" of true democracy during the past half-century.'[100]

In this harmonious vision of East African history, there is of course no place for violent, undemocratic and ungentleman-like intrusions such as the Mau Mau uprising.

In *The Road to Independence*, C.R.V. Bell is even more outspoken. When analyzing the Maji–Maji rebellion in Tanzania he writes for example: 'It is easy to say that the tribes rebelled because they did not like the severe rule of the Germans, and because they did not want to work on their plantations. But, as was to be the case with Mau Mau nearly fifty years later, there was more to it than this. Maji-Maji was un uprising of the forces of old Africa, of witchcraft and taboos, and of the traditions of communal tribal life against the new forces from Europe; against the idea that an individual was both more and less than part of his tribe.'[101]

By this historically unjustifiable comparison between Mau Mau and the Maji-Maji uprising, Mr. Bell skilfully suggests that the

European 'back to bush and savagery'-line is still an important element for explaining the revolt. Moreover, Mr. Bell suggests time and again that Mau Mau retarded Kenya's development ('There might have been years of very great prosperity throughout East Africa had it not been for the... Mau Mau troubles and the series of events which led to the exile of the Kabaka of Buganda'[102]), and at the end of his book he clearly tries to make us believe that Mau Mau has been of little significance in Kenya's march towards independence, when he writes: '*In spite of Mau Mau*, the British Government was determined to press forward with its plans for further constitutional development'.[103] This baffling conclusion runs counter to all the historical evidence we now have on the role of Mau Mau in Kenya's struggle for Independence. Unfortunately it must be quite difficult for secondary school children to see through this historiographical smokescreen.

Seen in the light of these facts one can understand why pro-Mau Mau parliamentarians like Mr. Kanja regularly plead that 'we must start teaching our children about the rebirth of our nation and they must be taught about those great men, ... so that they may feel proud and know that they are free'.[104]

There is, however, a possibility that things will change considerably in the near future. In *Zamani*, a handbook of East African History edited by B. A. Ogot and J. A. Kieran, which is also one of the recommended books for the higher forms of Kenya secondary schools, Professor Ogot gives already a much more balanced and modern view of Mau Mau. Although he still does not supply a detailed analysis of the whole phenomenon, he at least recommends to 'those who regard "Mau Mau" as an atavistic escape from modernity or as a barbarous tribal cult' to ponder the facts that Africans have their own dignity, and 'that they are jealous of it',[105] and he concludes that it is 'important to remember... that the shock of "Mau Mau" had created the right atmosphere in that the Imperial Power was now willing to talk with the African leaders'.[106]

This at any rate is a first step towards some kind of rehabilitation of the Mau Mau revolt in history books and the situation in the 'field' or rather in the classroom actually is probably even better than it appears on paper, i.e. from the Inspectorate's Book Lists. General China's '*Mau Mau*' *General*, although not recommended by the Ministry of Education, apparently has been bought by some schools and is used in history classes[107] although it is impossible to say by how many teachers. As the history teachers have some freedom in their choice of books, it is quite possible that they also use other books giving a more favourable image of Mau Mau like Rosberg and Nottingham's *Myth of Mau Mau*, which is, in fact, recommended by the Ministry for teacher's libraries. It should also be pointed out that the newly published E.A.A.C.E. History Syllabus 'Africa: National Movements and the New States', explicitly mentions the Mau Mau movement under the heading 'The struggle for self-Government'. As one of my informants at the Ministry of Education said: 'The syllabus in itself in no way affects comment on the Mau Mau movement but it does give it recognition as a movement which was part of the struggle for self-government.'

E. Some partial myths

The word 'partial' is not used here in the sense of dishonest, but rather to refer to myths or outlines of myths that only concern part of the Mau Mau history or that are only pushed by or current among specific and limited groups of people in Kenya. Several of these myths already exist in present day Kenya or are in the process of being created.

Regional legends

I do not have much information about this, but I did get the impression in Kenya that, at least among the common villagers in Kikuyuland, the myth of Mau Mau is often a 'split up' myth, that while people are very well acquainted with the facts of their local history during the Emergency, they know only a few rather loosely connected facts about the Mau Mau revolt in general. This seems to be the case in Murang'a (Fort Hall) District where some inhabitants know in great detail about the struggle of General Kago, the local Mau Mau hero, but are not very knowledgeable about Dedan Kimathi's struggle in Nyeri, only a few dozen miles up north, although they always admit in the end that Kimathi was the supreme commander, a sort of 'prime minister', of the Mau Mau revolt. In Embu District too, a local hero, General Kubukubu, seems to enjoy great renown, and it would be very interesting if detailed studies by Kikuyu-speaking scholars were undertaken to unearth the different kinds of myths current in different parts of Kikuyuland.

The fact that regional legends of Mau Mau do exist is in itself quite normal. As Dr. Barnett demonstrated in his *Mau Mau from Within*, the Mau Mau armies have always been organized on a regional basis and often operated on a sublocational level only. There were some overall Mau Mau Generals like Dedan Kimathi in Nyandarua Forest and General China on Mount Kenya who tried hard to give the Mau Mau revolt some semblance of unity, but for most of the Emergency period their leadership was only nominal, and the contacts between armed groups from different districts were infrequent if not non-existent. Given this 'split-up' character of the Mau Mau armies in the past, the existence of 'split-up' regional myths today is not in itself very amazing.

Mau Mau heroes

It is also interesting to analyze briefly the image of the few 'nation-wide' Mau Mau leaders who have been active during the Emergency and who were, in order of importance: Dedan Kimathi, Stanley Mathenge, and Waruhiu Itote (General China).

As far as Dedan Kimathi is concerned the situation is quite clear. As the nominal leader of all the Mau Mau Armies and as the man who laid down his life for the Independence of his country (he was executed by the British in 1957), he has become the personification of the armed struggle, and his image is very positive indeed. In nine out of ten cases his name is quoted when people want to single out a Mau Mau hero, and he is the only forest fighter who has a street named after him in Nairobi. His memorial will probably become the national Mau Mau monument if the plans of the Nairobi City Council, which we mentioned earlier, finally materialize. He is not only described almost everywhere as a 'brave and valiant fighter for freedom and a great leader of his people in the forest',[108] his admirers also almost invariably stress his kindness and gentleness. 'He was such a nice man,' a lady from North Tetu, where Kimathi lived, said to me, almost with tears in her eyes. J. M. Kariuki also explicitly mentions the fact that people who have known Kimathi thought him 'a very gentle, kindly man'.[109] In 1971 in Nairobi, I even met a boy of about fifteen years of age, also from North Tetu Division, who was apparently convinced that Kimathi, not Mr. Kenyatta, today would have been the President of Kenya if the British had not killed him. 'He was a big fighter, not Kenyatta,' was the principal argument used by this informant to give weight to his thesis. I do not know if this opinion is shared by many people in Kenya, but it is certainly symptomatic of the high esteem in which Kimathi is held by many Kikuyu today.

The case of Stanley Mathenge, second only to Kimathi in Nyandarua Forest and the undisputed leader of the Mau Mau forces from Othaya Division in Nyeri District, is a little bit more complex. Although Kimathi more or less monopolizes the publicity given to Mau Mau heroes, Mathenge also comes out very positively. A self-help secondary school in his home village in Mahiga location has been called after him, and several Cabinet Ministers referred to him in Parliament as a 'very distinguished person' having played a 'very patriotic role' in the struggle for Uhuru,[110] and a 'gallant freedom fighter'.[111]

There is, however, a problem with Mathenge. According to D.L. Barnett he was last seen in Nyandarua Forest in September 1955 and then disappeared.[112] His body has never been found and nobody knows for sure what has happened to him. As many forest fighters from the Nyandarua Armies have tried at the end of 1955 to break out of the forest in a desperate bid to reach Ethiopia or the Sudan, through the barren desert of the Northern Frontier Province, and as some of them indeed managed to reach their destination, it is no wonder that there are persistent rumours in Kenya that Stanley Mathenge is still alive and in hiding somewhere in Ethiopia or the Southern Sudan.

According to some articles in the *Daily Nation* in January 1971, his wife and his son Peter Miruigi Mathenge, are entirely convinced that these rumours are based on truth and that Mathenge will come back to Kenya some day. They both claim to have received visits of emissaries sent by Mathenge to inform them about his plans and his whereabouts.[113] His son even came to Embakasi Airport on the 15th of January 1971, because he was convinced that his father would arrive by plane on that day.[114]

Nobody knows for sure why Mathenge did not return. Some sources maintain that he might be unaware of the fact that Kenya achieved its Independence in 1963.[115] A lot of details in the press-reports published so far are certainly quite contradictory and I personally doubt whether Mathenge is really still alive. Most people I have spoken to are convinced of his death and Mr. Karimi, the *Daily Nation* reporter who covered the Mathenge story at the beginning of 1971, was also rather sceptical about the whole affair. Although he tried very hard to trace General Mathenge, he was never even able to meet the alleged 'emissaries' of the Mau Mau hero. However, some very knowledgeable people on Mau Mau are less definite on this issue: They think that Mathenge might indeed still be alive and that he might have personal reasons for not coming back.

Up till now the Kenya Government has not done much to find Mathenge. In 1962, before Kenya's Independence, Dr. Wayaki, now the Deputy-Speaker of Parliament, was sent to Ethiopia on behalf of the new political leaders of Kenya in order to contact the escaped forest-fighters and to persuade them to come home. He did indeed meet some of them, and was informed of rumours about Mathenge living in Ethiopia but further research proved unfruitful. Since then the Kenya Government has regularly announced that it is ready to welcome Mathenge back home and that it will even send a plane to fetch him,[116] but it has refused to launch a big search for him as long as new, concrete and detailed information is not forthcoming.

There is of course the eventuality of Mathenge's myth becoming a legend of the lost and hidden leader who will come back some day to rescue his people from injustice or tyranny, a sort of African Barberossa. Although the eventuality of such a legend should not be excluded beforehand (an article in the *Kenya Mirror* on the Mau Mau Legend mentioned the case of the Indian Patriot Chandra Bose who died in an airplane crash after the second world war and concluded: 'Even now millions in India still believe that he is alive... Some Indians believe that he is in the hiding waiting to emerge to give them new leadership'(!)[117]), there are actually no signs that it already exists or that it is in the process of being created. After all, the Kikuyu, in Kenya today, are one of the best catered for ethnic groups and as long as President Kenyatta is in power, they do not need legendary heroes to rescue them. If ever the situation changes and the Kikuyu become a forgotten and neglected group, then the myth of Mathenge might well take another form and eventually become a danger to the established authorities. At the moment, however, the prospects of such a situation ever occurring are dim if not non-existent.

We have seen what happened in the Mau Mau legend to a dead hero, Dedan Kimathi, and we have seen what happened to a hero who disappeared without leaving a trace. The third important leader of the Mau Mau Armies, Waruhiu Itote, better known as General China, is still alive and his case is particularly interesting. The fact is that China, although he has been one of the few forest fighters who has been given an important post in the Kenya administration after Independence,[118] today leads a very discreet and inconspicuous life. His personal files in the archives of the Kenya newspapers are extremely and amazingly thin because he is almost never mentioned in the press at all. No myths or legends seem to have been created around his person and he never poses as *the* leader of the forest fighters. The only time he briefly left his (self-imposed?) anonymity was in May 1967, when his autobiography was launched by the East African Publishing House, but even then press comments were sober and factual.

One might well ask why General China does not play a more important role in politics and in the legend of Mau Mau? Several reasons come to mind. The first one was suggested to me by some Kikuyu informants who thought that China, compared to Dedan Kimathi and Stanley Mathenge, did not stay in the forests for a very long time and, for this reason, cannot claim to be a really outstanding Mau Mau hero. Although it is true that China, who was arrested as early as January 1954, only stayed in the forest for about 15 months, his role in the Mount Kenya Army, which was quite well organized under his command, had been very important during this period. I am therefore inclined to be dissatisfied with such a simple explanation.

Another possibility I have pondered is that General China might be considered by some Mau Mau fighters as a traitor or at least as a controversial personality not eligible for hero-worship. After his arrest, China, in fact, helped the Colonial Administration by trying to contact the remaining forest fighters and persuade them to accept an official surrender offer, which gained for him a commutation of his death sentence into life imprisonment. Karari Njama goes even further and suggests that 'China must have revealed most of our secrets and plans to the Government which resulted in a complete destruction of our communications and supplies'.[119] In his *Memoirs* China, in his turn, goes to great pains to prove that he did not betray the forest fighters, that his role during the surrender talks was a very positive one, and that his deeds were, in fact, approved by Dedan Kimathi and all the other important Mau Mau leaders.[120]

Although China's role may eventually give rise to some argument among future historians, I did not gain the impression during my stay in Kenya that he is actually suspected by the majority of his compatriots of having betrayed the Mau Mau cause. The most plausible explanation for his discreet behaviour is probably that the ruling team in Kenya has offered him a sort of tacit deal and that he owes his actual administrative position in a way to his effacement in politics and in public life. In the actual political and socio-cultural configuration in Kenya, one can very well imagine that the more dead a Mau Mau hero is, the easier it is for the Government to accord him a hero's treatment. For the sake of national unity a living Mau Mau hero, who insisted on being treated as such, would be a great embarrassment, and it is quite possible that General China was informed that he can only be assured of his administrative career as long as he does not involve himself with politics. A last possibility would be that Mr. Itote is a staunch and sincere supporter of President Kenyatta who is convinced that the President could well do without competition from irksome Mau Mau heroes bent on public careers on their own. A combination of these last two reasons does not seem impossible.

An Asian myth

The only Kenya newspaper, that ever published a 'Mau Mau Special' is, to my knowledge, the *Kenya Mirror*.[121] It is also the only magazine that really becomes lyrical if not plainly hysterical when the subject of Mau Mau is brought up in its columns, which has been frequently the case since its inception somewhere in 1968. Let me just quote a few lines of an article entitled 'Who was Kimathi!', an article that produces no new facts, but that certainly describes the known facts in a way that is rather unusual in Kenya today: 'It is no longer in doubt that he was the brain behind the

Mau Mau uprising and that it was Dedan Kimathi who made the colonialists lick their own boots... Already he is a legend. Even before his death, he captured the imagination of the Africans and was respected by other international freedom movements. He was keenly aware of African political agitation and with his vast reading (sic) had acquired sufficient knowledge to understand the political reality of the country'.[122]

The interesting point here is that the *Kenya Mirror* is edited by a Kenya citizen of Asian descent and that the magazine is clearly meant to voice the opinions of the more 'progressive' part of the Asian population and to defend the special interests of this group. Why is it that an 'Asian' magazine is by far the most active in boosting the image of the Mau Mau fighters and why does it create this 'Asian' myth of Mau Mau?[123] In order to answer this question one has to take into account that the legend of Mau Mau, as it is presented in the *Kenya Mirror*, has two sides. First it glorifies the Mau Mau revolt, praising it to the skies as a breath-taking, marvelous saga enacted by almost superhuman heroes. Second it underlines again and again the Asian contribution to the revolt emphasizing facts like: The Asian lawyers that defended Mr. Kenyatta at Kapenguria; the intervention of Mr. K.P. Shah and other Asians in favour of Kenyatta during the Emergency[124]; the arms Asians allegedly supplied to the Mau Mau fighters; and the educational assistance they seem to have given to some of Kimathi's children.

One may conclude then that the *Kenya Mirror* is definitely trying to help the Kenya Asians to climb the Mau Mau band-wagon when it suggests that Asians were intimately associated with the movement in all its stages and that they actively participated in all the important events in Kenya's history like, for example, the liberation of Mr. Kenyatta. The reason for this is quite clear. The Asians of Kenya are actually in a very delicate position because they are considered by many Africans as a sort of second-class citizens, not really loyal to Kenya and exploiting the African population. For many of them the menace of deportation is quite real and what happened recently in Uganda can certainly not be reassuring to them. In these circumstances it becomes important for Asians to prove that they do belong to Kenya's history and that they did play a role in the struggle for Uhuru. The Asian myth of Mau Mau has to be seen in this light, although it must be said that the editor of the *Kenya Mirror* does take some risks if one considers the ambivalent feelings many Kenyans still harbour on the subject of Mau Mau.[125]

F. Conclusions

We have seen that Mau Mau during the last ten years has been played down in the public life of Kenya and that it has been 'sacrificed' for reasons of State and high politics. In some cases these reasons were quite honourable. President Kenyatta certainly was right when he made Kenya's national unity one of the cornerstones of his policy. He was also right when he insisted that the vicious circle of violence and counterviolence should not be reopened again in independent Kenya by seeking vengeance on the ex-Home Guards. I feel, however, that in the process of 'getting Kenya's history wrong' the tendency has been to play down Mau Mau too readily and unnecessarily so, and that even now, some new interpretations of Mau Mau as a historical phenomenon are not yet sufficiently known in Kenya.

I think that an interpretation of Mau Mau which takes into consideration its fundamental ambiguity might help to facilitate its integration into Kenya's history. I have developed these points elsewhere and I will only sketch them very briefly here.[126]

One of the most important questions people ask about Mau Mau is whether it was a tribal or a nationalist movement? I think that it is difficult to argue that Mau Mau was a nationalist movement in the classical sense of the term, and I feel myself that the African myth of Mau Mau goes much too far regarding this point, but I do not think that in the case of Mau Mau tribal should be *opposed* to nationalist, as it seems to be by many people.

Mau Mau was a tribal movement, but as a tribal movement it was not hostile to other ethnic groups in Kenya. It was rather a case of 'tribalism serving the Nation'. When Dedan Kimathi, for example, proposed to the Nyandarua forest fighters to found a 'Kenya Young Stars Association' of which they would all become members, he introduced his idea by saying that one day Jesus had spoken to his disciples in the following way: 'You are the light of the world... Let your light shine unto all.' 'We get light from the

84

sun, moon and stars,' said Kimathi. 'Now, since the government has taken away our sun, Jomo Kenyatta, and the moon, all the other political leaders – and even all the big stars have been arrested – only the *young stars* are left shining over the country… As Jesus has told his disciples, I tell you. You are the KENYA YOUNG STARS; keep on shining till the Sun and the Moon are released.'[127]

It is clear then that the leaders of the armed groups in the forest did not consider themselves as the real political leaders of the country and that their revolt was in a way a *revolt by procuration*, at least in their own eyes. That this was not just false modesty and idle words is shown by the answer given by General Kareba of the Mount Kenya army to the Kenya Government's surrender offer in January 1954: 'Our demands are Independence and land… and if the Government wishes for peace, our leaders, now in detention, must be released. *They are the politicians and can argue for our national Independence.* If this is done, the Forest Fighters will stop the war.'[128] A similar answer came from Dedan Kimathi and the Aberdare groups: 'Finally, we would like to meet Mr. Jomo Kenyatta or his representative… Mr. Chief Koinange, Mr. James Beauttah, Mr. E.W. Mathu, M.L.C., Mr. W.W.W. Awaori, M.L.C., and Mr. W. Odede, M.L.C…. There will be no negotiation talks in the absence of the above mentioned people.'[129]

The Mau Mau movement, although largely a Kikuyu movement by recruitment and in terms of its symbols and ceremonies, thus wanted to serve a group of political leaders – some of them Kikuyu, others not – about whose national outlook there can be no doubt. I think this proves sufficiently that in the end the Mau Mau fighters thought more in national terms than in tribal terms, and for this reason I am convinced that the question of whether Mau Mau was a tribal or a national movement is a faulty one. Mau Mau was both.

The same applies to the question whether Mau Mau was a modern or a traditional movement. Here again it can be said that Mau Mau was a traditional movement in so far as it used traditional Kikuyu symbols and beliefs, as well as ways of fighting and of organizing people. These traditional aspects of Mau Mau, however, were not ends in themselves but a means to an end in the struggle for a new Kenya. Since the Mau Mau freedom fighters had no other means at their disposal, they logically fell back on tradition. Their goals were largely modern, because they fought for the political programme Kenyatta and the other Kenya African Union leaders stood for. In so far as their movement was traditional, it was rather a case of *traditionalisme par excès de modernité*, as Jeanne Favret would say.[130]

If these interpretations of Mau Mau as a ambiguous, two-sided phenomenon became current in Kenya, it would be easier to assign to the movement its rightful place in the history of East Africa, although one problem would still remain, namely the difficulty for non-Kikuyu to come to a complete identification with the revolt.

3 Mau Mau in Literature and in the Popular Tradition

> 'Yes they are, we are all, a confused ge-
> neration ... a generation of confusion.'[1]

A. The forest fighters in fiction

To anyone familiar with French or Dutch literature, it is something of a shock to discover that Kenya has hardly any 'resistance-litera-ture'. In France and in Holland there appeared, during the first few years after the Second World War, several books which glorified the deeds of the resistance fighters who fought the Germans, and in many of these books like *L'Armée des Ombres* by Joseph Kessel and *Le grand Voyage* by Jorge Semprum for France, or *Die van Ons* by Willi Corsari for Holland, no doubt is left about the au-thors' sympathies. All characters are described in either black or white and the resistance fighters, men and women, are portrayed as heroes. In none of these novels is there a shadow of doubt about the correctness of their actions. In Semprun's stories, for example, the murder of a German or a traitor, is depicted as something completely normal and natural, a reputable act, provoking no, or only slight feelings of guilt.[2]

No such equivalent examples exist in Kenya. Barring one excep-tion, there are no novels at all in Kenya dealing with the fight in the forest as the main or central theme. How should one account for this? According to James Ngugi, this is simply a question of a generation gap. The first Kenya African novel that was ever pub-lished, only dates from 1964. Moreover, all Kenya writers are young men. They were at most schoolboys during the Emergency, who were themselves not directly and actively engaged in the free-dom fight. As writers generally create out of their own experiences, it is only natural that the Kenya novelists do not write about the forest fighters, but, if they write about the Emergency at all, build their work around the effects of the revolt on the civilian population in the Kikuyu Land Unit or in the towns, effects with which they are personally acquainted.[3]

I do not think this is entirely convincing. Although it is a fact that many writers deal mostly with what they have personally undergone, this is not always true, and Mr. Ngugi is himself a case in point. The pages where he describes life in a Kenya detention camp in his novel *A Grain of Wheat* are, in my opinion, among the best he ever wrote, and yet, as far as I know, Mr. Ngugi has never been in such a camp himself.[4] There must be other reasons for this absence of forest fighters' novels, because I do not think that it is purely accidental, as it is probably no accident either that one can find in Kenya children books and adolescent literature on Anna the Air Hostess, Pamela the Probation Officer, Hamisi's Safari, and Peter Mathu who becomes a Flying Doctor, but not on Njoroge the Freedom Fighter or Mumbi the Forest Nurse.[5] A more detailed analysis of the novels written by Kenya Africans and set in the Emergency days may help us to find a better answer to our problem.

'Ordeal in the Forest'

Godwin Wachira's *Ordeal in the Forest* is the only exception to the rule we discussed at the beginning of this chapter. The main theme of this novel is indeed the life of a group of freedom fighters in the forest and later on in detention camps. However, it does not belong to the 'resistance literature' in the sense we conceive of this term, because all through the book the author refuses, or is unable, really and completely to identify with his heroes. All characters and events are in fact described from outside and the image of Mau Mau remains confused. This may be partly due to lack of talent, *Ordeal in the Forest* being Mr. Wachira's first and up till now his only novel. But I am convinced that the confusion that reigns in the story springs first and foremost from the contradictions in Mr. Wachira's own mind.

The lack of identification with the Mau Mau movement is particularly evident in the first part of the book where the author describes the pre-emergency days of some of his characters who will later on become important Mau Mau leaders in the forest.

Although some of the less important among them are presented as intelligent and congenial men and women, the two main characters are painted almost entirely in negative terms. Mrefu, the future elder 'Mau Mau statesman' appears here as a violent man, a teacher who beats his pupils unmercifully, a real sadist, and also as an entirely insincere and false personality. As for Nundu, who will become the most important Mau Mau leader in the forest, he is even worse: He is pictured as a liar, a petty thief and a hooligan, 'a self-centred, conceited brute', as the author puts it.[6] His only reason for adhering to the upcoming Mau Mau movement seems to be self-interest: 'I only want to be a big man, the biggest man in the country and nothing and no one is going to stop me.'[7] Other minor Mau Mau members show similar feelings, when they explain their reasons for being members of Mau Mau.[8]

In the second part of the book which deals with the first years of the Emergency and with the actual fighting in the forest, the tone changes slightly and Wachira seems to make a real effort to accommodate the revolt and its actions. Here at last he takes some pride in the movement, and even suggests in a few passages that the role of Mau Mau in the liberation of Kenya will later on be considered of historical importance. Even the leaders of the revolt, who during the first part of the story were described from a distance as somewhat curious but rather repulsive insects, now become more positive and appealing. About Mrefu the author says, for example: 'His dominating personality and courage together with a gift for restoring peace between warring factions, and his teachers' training, gave him the position of guide, philosopher and friend to the youths, thus making him a natural commander.'[9] Nundu also becomes much more of a positive character and the author praises his 'courage and tenacity',[10] and his leaders' capacities: 'He was a genius when it came to organizing'.[11]

However, before we hurriedly declare *Ordeal in the Forest* to be a forest-fighter novel in the sense of 'resistance literature', two remarks must be made. First of all, nowhere does Wachira explain why and how such positive changes suddenly take place in the personality of his main characters. They do not *become* better men, they all of a sudden *are* better men. One gets the feeling that this concentration on telling a story, in which there are many unrelated episodes and people, at the expense of internal character development, is fairly typical of the genesis of many African novelists. It would probably have been more acceptable if these changes took place because of their allegiance to the Mau Mau movement or if the author had stated that their belonging to Mau Mau itself was responsible for this change. But no correlation or connexion is established between the two phenomena which is one of the main reasons why *Ordeal in the Forest* does not qualify as 'resistance literature'.

Secondly, even in this part of the book, the positive aspects of the Mau Mau heroes present only one side of the picture. At the height of the struggle in the forest, Mrefu and Nundu remain essentially ambivalent characters, who never become completely acceptable and whom one can neither love nor admire. Here is, for example, the description of Nundu's behaviour when he is made a Field-Marshal of the Mau Mau Army: 'He could not contain his joy at his promotion, and jumped up and down like a little boy who has been given the toy of his dreams... For once he seemed almost human. Too soon, however, his aggressive nature reasserted itself... His breast swelling with pride, he strutted out of his cave like a turkey cock.'[12] A few pages later we learn that 'he had turned into a dictator,'[13] and become a 'fierce brute'.[14] Wachira also insists heavily on certain negative aspects of the fight in the forest like the internal quarrels of the leaders, the use of drugs, especially before battle, by the freedom fighters and the superstitious beliefs that were current in the forest.

I do not wish to argue that the leaders of the forest-fighters were in reality 'knights without fear or reproach'. They certainly were not and they indeed had many of the negative traits Wachira ascribes to them. I too am well aware that the Mau Mau Army has always been torn apart by internal strife, and that many of the Mau Mau privates and even generals were superstitious and did sometimes use drugs. I only argue that Wachira, being 'neutral' and 'uninvolved', is unable to discount the negative sides of the revolt and give an overall positive picture of the movement. It is only at the very end of his novel, when Mrefu is discharged from jail, after having rather lamentably failed in detention to live up to his reputation as an important Mau Mau leader, that Wachira again strikes a positive note. Meditating about the deeper meaning of his involvement in the armed struggle Mrefu concludes: 'You know, our physical fight wasn't a complete failure. You wait and see. In the years to come, our fight for freedom will be known as something noble and worthwhile; and this fight, which we have sadly lost at the moment, will prove to be the decisive point, the point where the white man started to think about our *Uhuru*.'[15] Here again the author seems to identify with the revolt, but the book nevertheless ends on a hesitant note, with a sentence which I believe is typical of the whole way the Mau Mau movement has been treated by Kenya writers. 'Yes they are, we are all, a confused generation... a generation of confusion', says Mrefu on the last page of *Ordeal in the Forest*.[16] Hesitation and confusion, these terms most aptly describe Wachira's own attitude towards Mau Mau, and the same terms apply to some of his colleagues.

James Ngugi and the forest-fighters
Two other Kenya writers have treated the theme of the forest fighters, although as a sideline. The case of James Ngugi is particularly interesting here because, one can perceive a very explicit change over a period of time in the way the theme is handled in his work. In his first novel *Weep not Child* which focusses on the experiences of an adolescent schoolboy during the Emergency, Ngugi is still almost a completely impartial describer of what happened in Kenya during these dark days. 'In fact he tries hard to balance the brutality of the home guards with the violence of the Mau Mau', one of his critics rightly says about this book.[17] The forest-fighters are represented by Boro, one of the brothers of Njoroge, the main hero, and although almost nothing is said about Boro's life in the forest, the most important passage devoted to this subject, a dialogue between Boro and one of his lieutenants, clearly gives a rather negative and even nihilistic image of the Mau Mau Army:

"Don't you believe in anything?"

"No. Nothing. Except revenge."

"Return of the lands?"

"The lost land will come back to us maybe. But I have lost too many of those whom I loved for land to mean much to me. It would be a cheap victory."

Boro was a bit more communicative as he sat with his lieutenant on a look-out a few miles from their new hide-out... Boro had always told himself that the real reason for his flight to the forest was a desire to fight for freedom. But this fervour had soon worn off. His mission became a mission of revenge. This was the only thing that could now give him fire and boldness...

"And freedom?", the lieutenant continued.

"An illusion. What freedom is there for you and me?"

"Why then do we fight?"

"To kill. Unless you kill, you'll be killed. So you go on killing and destroying. It's a law of nature...

"But don't you think there's something wrong in fighting and killing unless you're doing so for a great cause like ours?"

"What great cause is ours?"

"Why, Freedom and the return of our lost heritage."

"Maybe there's something in that. But for me Freedom is meaningless unless it can bring back a brother I lost. Because it can't do that, the only thing left to me is to fight, kill and rejoice at any who falls under my sword..."[18]

This is clearly a distant echo of the way in which Max Gluckman pictured Mau Mau in his essay *The Magic of Despair:* 'Mau Mau is a nihilistic movement of desperation – kill and be killed.'[19] We will see later on that *Weep not Child* is in every aspect a rather ambivalent book, and that it is difficult to find out Mr. Ngugi's stand on Mau Mau if one only takes into account this first fruit of his talent.

However, in his third novel, *A Grain of Wheat*, Ngugi is much more explicit on the whole issue, and he seems to have undergone a real personal evolution during the few years since he wrote *Weep not Child*. The main theme of this book, which we shall analyze later on in more detail, is the moral and personal problems of a group of typical non-combating Kikuyu villagers during the Emergency and up till Independence Day. However, the most important forest-fighter in *A Grain of Wheat*, although he only makes a few direct appearances, is present in the background throughout the whole story, one of the main themes of the book in fact being who betrayed this man, Kihika.

Moreover, unlike Boro in *Weep not Child*, Kihika is painted as a real hero, a man of true grit who was implacable in his mission, a man whose moral superiority over all the other characters in the novel is unquestioned. 'He was a priest... a high priest of this our freedom', one of the other characters in the book says about him,[20] and one of Ngugi's favourable critics concludes: 'Only one major character in the book appears to be free from guilt, and this is Kihika... *A Grain of Wheat* pays tribute to those who fought, however criss-crossed the moral threads may be.'[21]

There is also one secondary character in Ngugi's last novel that is free from guilt: General R., another forest-leader who was once Kihika's close lieutenant and who survived the war. Although he does not rise to the somewhat superhuman dimensions of Kihika, he too is described as a strong personality, an intelligent and nice man who does not seem to know what failure means. It is clear then where Ngugi's sympathies lie, but we shall see that even in this book, he is still too uninvolved to be able to write a real 'resistance novel' in the sense we defined this category in the beginning of this chapter.

Kahiga's Heroes

The only Kenya writer who, in my opinion, could possibly write such a novel, is Samuel Kahiga. In *Potent Ash*, he published in fact two short stories which come very close to being resistance literature. In these stories, forest-fighters or their helpers in the Kikuyu Reserves are the main heroes, and their image is definitely positive, although the author does not conceal their weaknesses. In Kahiga's case however, these weaknesses do not damage the overall positive picture of the forest fighters, because in a way, the author is so convinced of the moral superiority of his Mau Mau heroes and the justice of their cause, that a few negative shades do not matter anymore. Kahiga can afford to mention them for they only make his heroes more credible.

The first one I shall analyse is the story of *Esther*, a Kikuyu woman coming home late at night one day during the Emergency, after having planned – this is only very skilfully suggested by the author, not stated in so many words – an attack on the Home Guard post of her village which will be executed by a group of forest fighters later on the same night. When she enters her hut, she discovers that her mother-in-law and her daughter, anxious about her absence, have sent her youngest son to inquire about her at the neighbours and at the Home Guard post. Esther disappears again into the night in order to try to save her son, but too late:

The boy is inside the fort at the moment the forest fighters set fire to the post. The Mau Mau Army certainly does not obtain an 'easy victory', and one cannot say that Kahiga only presents the Mau Mau struggle as a gay and happy war. However, he is clearly on the side of Esther and does everything to portray her favourably, for example, in this passage where he describes her as her son sees her:

'She often went out to see a neighbour. When his father raised protests saying it was dangerous she laughed at him. She was so strong and full of courage and fire. If she came in and found them sitting miserably round the fire, worrying over her, she would just burst out laughing.'[22] This is a characteristic description of the author's heroine. Elsewhere she clearly has the last word in a discussion with her rather cowardly and Home-Guard-orientated husband about some of the alleged Mau Mau crimes, a discussion also seen through the eyes of her son:

'His mother called the homeguards devils. Few of them, she always said, had the guts to face their real enemies. So they beat up innocent people.

"The terrorists are even more cowardly", his father had once replied.

"Who are they fighting, I want to know? The villages they have burnt! The innocent lives they have taken! Everywhere they go they kill their own because they can't get at the white people..."

... "The black people who have refused to take oaths are not their own", his mother had replied quietly.

"They are Europeans at heart. That is why they kill them."

"They kill innocent children too", his father had flashed back indignantly.

"Yes", his mother had replied calmly, "The larvae of the weevil must go with the parent".'[23]

By letting the mother have the last word and by underlining the calmness of her answers, the author gives the impression that he is on her side in this discussion, and that he himself is beyond the whole problem of Mau Mau crimes. He seems to accept these 'crimes' as a necessary part of a revolution of which one feels he is proud.

The same is true for *Departure at Dawn*, in which he describes a badly wounded forest fighter who is hiding in a abandoned store belonging to his brother, who still works as a farm-hand for a European lady, and who still cowers under the 'moral' superiority of the Europeans, as also his seventeen year old son, Karanja. Again, this is not a one-sided, heroic saga. Ndonga the wounded freedom fighter, is very ill and materially in a very bad position. However, his composure and self-possession compels the admiration of the reader.

'When a little insect hums around you, intruding upon your calm and peaceful meditations you absent-mindedly slap it against your leg, killing it', Ndonga says to his nephew. 'To the white race, we are insects. But Karanja, we have learnt to sting. So, my boy, sting.'[24] 'But Karanja felt that it would serve no purpose... Nobody's position would be improved. He would only become a hunted man like uncle Ndonga. He did not think that his uncle was a man to envy especially in his present situation.'[25]

This is the end of the discussion between Ndonga and Karanja, but as with Esther, the uncle in the end gets the last word. When Karanja brings him to the headman's office, because Ndonga is dying anyway and might find some relief of his sufferings in hospital, the headman does not even listen to a word of Karanja's story, but kills the defenceless terrorist off-hand with a rifle shot. It is very cleverly suggested by the author that Karanja will be arrested in his turn and probably accused of complicity with the forest fighters. 'Whether you sting or not', the author seems to say at the end of his story, 'you will get exactly the same treatment because you are but an African.' As I have said before, these two short stories come nearest to what I consider as 'resistance literature', and I hope that Mr. Kahiga will one day come back to the theme of the forest-fighters in a mature novel. The result could be very interesting, because Kahiga is certainly a talented writer.

B. The Emergency in fiction

As we have seen, not much is said in Kenya's youthful literature on the Mau Mau freedom fighters, and most of what has been said is of a hesitant and ambivalent nature. There are more novels about the period of the Emergency, that is about the life of the civilian population in the Kikuyu Land Unit at that time, but most of this literature, too, is rather ambiguous and clearly mirrors the confusion that reigns in Kikuyu thinking about Mau Mau and the Emergency. This is particularly the case with James Ngugi, today Kenya's most outstanding creative writer who, as one of his critics said, is, 'the champion of the little man: The little man close to the soil.'[26] Being the champion and the spokesman of the little man, Ngugi's hesitations are much more comprehensible than, for example, those of Godwin Wachira, in so far as they reflect the moral disarray of this little man, i.e. the non-fighting civilian in the reserves he represents and identifies with, and not necessarily those of the author.

It is also true, as we have seen in our analysis of the way in which he describes the forest-fighters in his books, that he underwent a striking personal evolution between his first novel and his work of maturity. In *Weep not Child* the characters are not only hesitant, but so also is Ngugi; in *A Grain of Wheat* some of the characters are still confused, but the author is much more lucid.

'Weep not Child'

In Ngugi's first novel, life during the Emergency is seen through the eyes of Njoroge, an intellectually brilliant but for the rest rather immature Kikuyu schoolboy, who constantly dreams about some vague 'mission in life' and for whom 'schooling... was the end of all living.'[27] In fact, Njoroge is a weak character, indulging in self-pity and escapism, and who throughout the whole book, never shows any sign of political consciousness. He only reacts to the events of the Emergency in so far as they interfere directly with his own petty existence, for example at the end of the book when he has to interrupt his schooling because of the alleged or real participation of some members of his family in the Mau Mau movement. What is true for Njoroge is also true for Mwihaki, the daughter of a Government Chief and Home Guard for whom he has a childlike love. They are both small human beings who do not participate in the events of their time and who have not the slightest control over them.

Quite logically they show themselves unable to adopt a personal and positive standpoint on the Mau Mau issue, their main reaction being that of escapism. 'I don't know what is happening', writes Mwihaki to Njoroge, after having mentioned some problems related to the Emergency, '... I am caught in it and if this goes on I feel as if I could go mad ... I am telling all this to show you how glad I am at the prospects of escaping away from it all.'[28] This indeed is the only conclusion to which our disturbed and unhappy lovers can come: 'We must go away. Kenya is no place for us.'[29] Of course, history catches up with them and they never get any chance to escape at all ... Characteristic for Njoroge's attitude, is also his reaction when he learns that the forest fighters are planning to burn down the government-approved school where he is a pupil. 'I thought Mau Mau was on the side of black people', he exclaims bitterly,[30] but the question why the Mau Mau leaders wanted to destroy government and missionary schools, at a time when all Kikuyu independent schools were forcibly closed down by the colonial authorities, apparently never enters his mind.

Was Ngugi, in 1963 when he wrote his novel, aware of this very legitimate question and did he have an answer to it? I am not quite sure. E. Hower, when evaluating Ngugi's first novel writes that: 'Ngugi's sensitivity to the human motives on both sides of the conflict is (to the European reader at least) one of his great strengths as a novelist', although he admits that, occasionally 'it gets in his way, and reduces some of his characters to positions of abject helplessness.'[31] I feel, however, that this sensitivity, at least in *Weep not Child*, is not a strength but a weakness and I tend to agree with A. Ravenscroft who thinks that 'Ngugi identifies the current of his own emotions too closely with his hero's; he has not yet mastered the achievement of creative objectivity.'[32] In my opinion, in 1963 James Ngugi had not yet learned to live with Mau Mau and to accept it as a part of the history of Kenya and of his people. In 1967, with the ripening of his talent, his weakness had become a strength as we shall see below.

'*A Grain of Wheat*'

This book does not describe the life of one Kikuyu family during the Emergency as seen through the eyes of an immature schoolboy, but the life of a whole Kikuyu village as seen by a mature writer i.e. James Ngugi himself. Although even this novel still has some weaknesses both in construction and in style, Ngugi here at least managed to take sufficient distance from his own creations and to achieve creative objectivity. '*A Grain of Wheat...*', says A. Ravenscroft, 'shows a great advance in Ngugi's development as an artist. There is no romantic self-indulgence; on the contrary, a far more rigorous looking at human problems and sufferings, a more successful integration of the personal dilemmas of his characters with wider social problems; ... Instead of sighing over his characters' failures, Ngugi now analyzes the reasons for their behaviour and gives us a compassionate yet realistic insight into human experience.'[33]

In *A Grain of Wheat* Ngugi in a way, draws up an inventory of the different ways of behaviour open to a Kikuyu during the Emergency, each of his main characters representing one of the possible choices that were open at the time. First of all there is Kihika, the freedom fighter, who stands at one end of the continuum. He is the man who already sided with Mau Mau long before the Emergency and who took to the forest as soon as the fighting broke out, leaving behind everything he loved, including his fiancée. He stands for courage and strength of personality, and he is, as we have seen before, the only character in Ngugi's novel who has no weaknesses and who has never failed, the only one without guilt and whom everybody admires.

Next to Kihika we have Gikonyo, the carpenter, who was a supporter of the Mau Mau movement before the Emergency and who has taken the oath of unity. Gikonyo, however, is a much weaker character than Kihika, and after having been imprisoned for some time in a detention camp, he becomes a 'traitor', the first one of his camp to 'confess' in order to be rehabilitated and sent home. In spite of Gikonyo's betrayal, however, the author does not condemn him but, on the contrary, cleverly analyzes why he succumbs under the pressure of the dull and desperate life in detention. Gikoyo's great 'weakness' is his love for Mumbi, his young wife, and it is because of her that he chooses to betray. Ngugi describes his homecoming in the following words: 'He did not feel victorious, less a hero. The green leaves were not for him. But then, Gikonyo did not want them. He only wanted to see his Mumbi and take up the thread of life where he had left it.'[34] Gikonyo is a very real and credible personality, symbolizing a type of behaviour which has probably characterized many Kikuyu men during the Emergency. How many of them have not tried to come to terms with the colonial rulers and to go through the 'pipeline' of rehabilitation as quickly as possible in order to be returned to their families?

With Mugo, the solitary farmer living without a wife or a family and almost without contacts with his neighbours in the village, we are already on the negative side of the continuum, although the reader does not know this throughout the greater part of the book, because he is at first presented to us as seen through the eyes of the other villagers who admire him for his behaviour during the Emergency. Mugo, in fact, was the only man who dared to interfere when a pregnant woman was whipped by a Home Guard during a compulsory collective work-party in his village, which landed him in a detention camp, where he became a legend because of his steadfast and unwavering attitude. He even took the lead during a hunger-strike of the detainees and did not yield when tortured. No wonder then that the villagers admired this seemingly modest and discreet man and that they wanted to make him a village chief and bestow upon him the honour of delivering the main speech during the Independence Day celebrations.

Gradually, however, the reader is led to the conclusion that there is something wrong with Mugo and that he may not quite be the hero other people see in him. It finally becomes clear that he not only held out in detention because he was a desperate man with nobody in the village waiting for him, certainly not a woman, as in the case of Gikonyo, but also that he had accepted the tortures and the beatings while in detention as a kind of punishment he deserved. He is in fact the man who betrayed Kihiga to the British. He is the man for whom everybody is searching and out of whom the villagers hope to force a confession during the Uhuru Day Celebrations. This is the irony of fate, that the man whom the villagers admire most and whom they are ready to make their chief is finally the betrayer of their forest hero.

Again, Ngugi does not judge or condemn his own creation, and at the end of the book Mugo shows himself capable of an act of great moral courage. When he finally accepts the invitation of the villagers to deliver the speech on Independence Day, he uses the occasion to denounce himself publicly as the Judas who betrayed Kihiga. Ngugi suggests that he is subsequently executed by General R. and the other surviving forest fighters, but the real verdict is pronounced by Gikonyo who says: 'He was a brave man, inside... He stood before much honour, praises were heaped on him. Tell me another person who would have exposed his soul for all the eyes to peck at ... Remember that few people in that meeting are fit to lift a stone against that man. Not unless I – we – too in turn open our hearts naked for the world to look at.'[35] This 'absolution' is typical of Ngugi's attitude throughout the whole book. Instead of condemning, he analyses the motives which impell his characters to act as they do, explaining their behaviour even if it is morally reprehensible.

In the case of Mugo the reason for his betrayal of Kihiga is that the latter wanted to try and drag him into the freedom struggle. Mugo, however, as a typical Ngugi-hero, is one of those people who think, without any reason, that they have an important mission in life and that they have to bide their time instead of getting involved in a chain of events that do not really concern them. When he is on his way to betray Kihiga to the District Commissioner he ponders: 'I am important. I must not die. To keep myself alive, healthy and strong – to wait for my mission in life – is a duty to myself, to men and women of tomorrow. If Moses had died in the reeds, who would ever have known that he was destined to be a great man?'[36] These vague dreams of Mugo have no link at all with reality but they tell us why he hated Kihiga who tried to coerce him into choosing another path.

Ngugi does not even condemn the behaviour of Karanja, as a Home Guard and a Government Chief, the exact opposite of Kihiga, but explains it on the basis of his hopeless love for Mumbi in whose proximity he wants to be when her husband, Gikonyo, is sent to detention; also out of his genuine conviction that the British are after all too strong to be defeated by Mau Mau. Ngugi even succeeds in letting us feel and understand Karanja's complete disarray when his European superior, whom he sees as a sort of infallible father-figure, leaves Kenya on the eve of Independence without even saying goodbye to him. Although his behaviour is never justified, and although he is always pictured as a negative character, Karanja finally inspires pity more than hatred or contempt. Even he has two sides. He is not only the traitor of the sacred cause of the Kenya Africans, but also the frustrated lover who longs for the sympathy and favours of Mumbi.

The Emergency, then, as seen by James Ngugi, is not a period which is seen only in terms of black and white, but a period in which black and white, good and bad, heroism and betrayals are intimately intertwined. In *A Grain of Wheat* 'the author's unwillingness to judge hardly any of his characters' is not due to any confusion in the ideas of Ngugi but, as E. Hower says: 'A refusal to make facile, politically expedient statements about the fate of the villagers and the nation.'[37] His comprehension and his understanding of the motives of both parties in the conflict, might however make it difficult for James Ngugi ever to focus one of his novels on the forest fighters. He is and probably will remain the champion of the hesitant little man trying to survive during the Emergency, rather than become the spokesman of the hero who resolutely chooses sides and brushes aside the subtle weighting of argument and counter-argument.

The theme of the return

'All of them longed for one day – the day of their return home. Then life would begin anew',[38] says one of James Ngugi's ex-detainees on his way home when musing on his experiences in detention. This theme of return certainly haunts Ngugi, as it does some other Kenya writers, and it is interesting here to analyze briefly the way it has been treated in literature, since it will provide us with an insight into the way in which Kenyans and especially Kikuyu villagers view Mau Mau and the Emergency. The most striking thing is that the emphasis is almost invariably on the discrepancy between the high hopes and the beautiful dreams nourished in detention and the grim reality facing the detainees on their return when they are forced to realize that during their absence life went on and that many things have changed adversely.

Ngugi himself has treated this subject no less than three times with varying success. In his play *The Wound in the Heart*, published in 1971, but probably written much earlier, the shock of the returning freedom fighter is the greatest. During his absence his wife had been raped by a white District Officer and on the day of his return she gives birth to the child of this forced union. In utter despair and shame, she commits suicide, while her husband dies the very same day prostrated over her dead body, probably out of sheer psychological shock.[39] I entirely agree with Mr. Tejani that the whole incident has a hollow ring and that the plot does great injustice to the subject.[40] In this play Ngugi still shows his unfamiliarity with the medium of drama and this work is mainly interesting as a sociological document, not as an example of creative art.

In *A Grain of Wheat* Ngugi returned to an almost similar theme, but this time with much more insight into human psychology, and with much more mastery in the construction and handling of dramatic events. We have seen before that, in this novel Gikonyo the carpenter, stands for those men who, although supporting the cause of Mau Mau in their heart, finally were unable to face the hardships of detention. Gikonyo, in particular, betrays Mau Mau and confesses his 'guilt' because he wants to be reunited with Mumbi, his beloved wife. When he comes home after six years, however, it is only to discover that he has betrayed Mau Mau in vain and that his wife feeds a child of the destestable Karanja, once his unhappy rival in love, who took advantage of his position as a Home Guard during his absence. Ngugi renders particularly well the almost animal despair of Gikonyo when he discovers this, and his mute, but violent reactions afterwards, when he refuses to take up married life again and treats his wife as a sort of despicable house-maid.

At the same time, the theme of return is also at the root of one of the greatest weaknesses of this novel. It is indeed rather unbelievable that the faithful Mumbi, who stayed pure for years and years during her husband's absence suddenly surrenders to Karanja when he tells her that her husband is at last going to be released. As D. Cook says: 'It is not that this is an impossible reaction on her part; but rather that the author seems to take it for granted as natural emotional logic which needs no explanation.'[41] I myself have the impression that Ngugi wants us to believe that Mumbi is rather confusedly convinced that it is Karanja's intervention which will help secure her husband's release, but I am not even sure that this interpretation is correct. Anyway, if this is what the author wanted to suggest, he failed in his excessive discretion.

In *The Return*, a short story of only seven pages, Ngugi has treated his favourite theme in the subtlest and the purest form. The story is simple: a detainee comes home, hoping for a 'hero's welcome', but in reality finds out that everybody in his village has thought of him as dead, because one of the members of his age-group has spread this lie with the deliberate intention of poaching his beautiful wife, in which he indeed succeeded. The story, however, ends on a positive note. The night after his return, Kamau, the ex-detainee, walks through the fields in order to clarify his ideas. More and more, he begins to feel that he will accept the changes that have come into his existence and he definitely veers towards a positive solution of his problems when he discovers that his old mother has followed him all night, because she feared that he might commit some act of despair: 'He looked at her and forgot all about himself. "Mother!" It was a softened voice full of emotion. He went towards her and took her by the arm. "Let's go home!", he murmured again. This was truly his "return", and as he peered into the future, as he became aware of the beauty of life in spite of his hardships, he could see no possibility of his going away again.'[42]

In *A Grain of Wheat* also, a positive conclusion is reached when Gikonyo finally forgives his wife, admits his own faults, and decides to start a new life with her:

'"Will you – will you come tomorrow!", he asked, unable to hide his anxiety and fear. He knew, at once, that in future he would reckon with her feelings, her thoughts, her desires – a new Mumbi. Again she considered his question for a little while. "All right. Maybe I shall come", she said and took her leave. She walked away with determined steps, sad but almost sure. He watched her until she disappeared at the door. Then he sank back to bed. He thought about the wedding gift, a stool carved from Muiri wood. "I'll change the woman's figure. I shall carve a woman big – big with child".'[43]

In another publication entitled *The Return*, a fragment of a play by J. Ngunjiri, the returning freedom fighter is a woman, not a man, but the situation she has to face is much the same and the woman in question, Gathoni, poses much the same eternal questions when coming home on Independence Day. Was Uhuru worth my suffering? What does Freedom mean to me who has been separated from my children for nine years and who will have to accept to live with the second wife my husband was forced to take in order to be able to raise my children? The human, personal problems are again in the centre, not the exaltation of the fight for freedom. The tone of the play is very well given in the following dialogue between Gathoni and one of the villagers she encounters on her way home:

Kamau: "You can be sure – your imprisonment, and the imprisonment of so many like you, was not in vain".

Gathoni: "Not in vain? For whom?"

Kamau: "For all of us."

Gathoni: "Not for me. I broke my home, deserted my children, ruined my whole life."[44]

And when Kamau tries to remind her of the general historical dimensions of the issue, by pointing out that sometimes, one individual has to suffer in order to save the whole community, Gathoni again falls back on her personal problems and exclaims bitterly: 'Yes! Oh, that's right. After all, only one woman – only one fighting woman – of course, I understand. But unluckily, the one woman was I, it was *me*.'[45]

In my opinion, this cry is characteristic of the way Mau Mau and the Emergency are treated in Kenya's literature: little heroism and resistance literature, but an almost exclusive concentration on the human problems of the participants in this great historical drama, be they members or sympathizers of the Mau Mau movement, fence-sitters, or even enemies and traitors. This, I think, is a strength... and a weakness at the same time.

C. Mau Mau in the popular tradition

Although I speak neither Kikuyu nor Swahili, and although my contacts with Kikuyu villagers have been limited, I would like briefly to treat the subject of Mau Mau in the popular tradition. The few impressions I have on this matter may be useful as a starting hypothesis for a better prepared scholar who, I hope, will one day examine this field more thoroughly.

What has struck me in Kenya, is how often, at all levels of the population, Kikuyu and non-Kikuyu alike, the subject of Mau Mau causes embarrassment. We have seen how true this is of the official circles in Kenya and we have analyzed the reasons for this. I would now like to try and find out if there are any specific reasons for this reluctance even among many Kikuyu villagers and peasants.

Mau Mau as a civil war

First of all we have to remember the way the colonial myth of Mau Mau has been impressed upon the Kikuyu mind. Tens of thousands of ordinary Kikuyu, men and women, have spent years and years in detention camps, where they have been exposed to an enormous

104

amount of brainwashing and propaganda, without being able to organize for themselves their mental defence. It is quite probable, that many Kikuyu suffer from the after-effects of the guilt-complexes created during this period. I have already mentioned before this problem of the interiorization of the colonial myth of Mau Mau by many Africans and I will not come back to it now, but would rather refer to Joram Wamweya's recent book: *Freedom Fighter*. It is indeed characteristic and significant that Wamweya, who was an enthusiastic member of Mau Mau and even a forest fighter for a short period, sometimes speaks about the Mau Mau movement in terms one would normally only use for the Mafia or Cosa Nostra, or some other gangster organization. Several times Mau Mau is referred to as the 'Council of the Perpetrators of Crime',[46] and the words 'terrorist', 'crime' and 'acts of terror' recur in Wamweya's story. This means that he, like many others, has at least swallowed part of the colonial myth and part of the colonial vocabulary related to Mau Mau, which is all the more revealing, since he never rejects his Mau Mau record, but, on the contrary, seems to be rather proud of it.

It must also be said that right from the start, Mau Mau has had the dimension of a civil war, a war of the Kikuyu have-nots, against those they called the 'Black Europeans', i.e. the rich African farmers and the government chiefs and headmen. The statistics on Mau Mau victims, indeed, tell their own tale: according to official sources only 32 European civilians were killed by the insurgents, as against no less than 1819 African civilians.[47] Although most of these Africans were killed not because they were Africans, but because they were seen as 'Black Europeans', i.e. traitors to the African cause, this killing of their own kind certainly has had a negative effect on the image of Mau Mau.

Already during the Emergency it was one of the most controversial and hotly debated Mau Mau issues as is shown by the 'Emergency' novels. We referred before to Samuel Kahiga's discussion between Esther and her husband, where Esther candidly and firmly defends the liquidation even of women and children and where she finally gets the last word.[48]

In another story in the same volume, Leonard Kibera introduces a Kikuyu peasant who is strongly against the British and even more against the Loyalists, but who at the same time, blames the freedom

105

fighters for being 'the impotent sons of the land who he claimed had lost the common, virile vision and were now slaughtering their own people aimlessly like a tribe of tired sadists.'[49] Other examples of discussions and reproaches of this kind can be cited from the work of James Ngugi, and there are vague indications that even today some ex-Mau Mau fighters are still afraid of accusations of this nature.

This image of the freedom fighters as killers of their fellow Africans, very probably explains part of the embarrassment of the Kikuyu people to talk about Mau Mau, and it is particularly interesting to note that even some Africans who are favourably disposed towards Mau Mau, have accepted in faith at least one part of the European legend of Mau Mau, namely that the forest fighters indiscriminately killed men, women and children. This, in reality, is a myth, as is shown by the facts. J. Wilkinson, a medical doctor, strongly hostile to Mau Mau, reported in July 1954 that, of the 1024 Mau Mau victims then known to the authorities, only 98 were females;[50] as for the Mau Mau victims admitted to Tumutumu hospital up till May 1954, he gives the following breakdown:[51]

Age Group	Men	Women	Total
Children	2	1	3
Adults	154	28	182
Old People	26	—	26
Total	182	29	211

The conclusion is quite simple: The freedom-fighters never slaugthered women and children in great numbers as some of the exponents of the colonial myth of Mau Mau would have us believe.

The freedom fighters as scapegoats

I have the impression that the Mau Mau fighters have not only been made 'responsible' for the killing of many Africans, but that during the second part of the revolt, the relations between them and the Kikuyu civilian population became generally strained. The reasons for the deterioration of this relationship are several and complex, but some of them come out quite clearly in Wamweya's Memoirs.

106

Speaking about the situation at the end of 1954, Wamweya first of all says: 'At about this time it became evident that people from the Reserves were forsaking the forest fighters. It became increasingly difficult to get either clothes or food from the people.'[52] In order to keep going, the forest fighters then had to decide to loot not only the property of Europeans and Loyalists, but also that of innocent villagers and even of Mau Mau sympathizers. 'This decision, however, was to bring very disastrous results for the cause. Reserve-dwellers did not appreciate the reasons for this change of tactics. As a result, their sympathy for the warriors was alienated... Henceforth freedom-fighters were treated like wild animals by everybody.'[53] Later on, Wamweya again mentions the difficult relations between the warriors and the villagers and gives another reason for this state of affairs: 'By this time (1955–56) the forest fighter was out of favour with all sides – with the colonialists and with the *wananchi*. We dared not be seen by anybody, for we were sure to be reported by all who saw us. *To those in the Reserves, a good forest fighter was a dead one.* This had come about as a result of those forest fighters who had been captured and who had no wit to create make-believe confessions. They had betrayed all those that had aided them, and put them into serious trouble.'[54]

From other sources, we also know that at that time, the freedom-fighters and not the colonialists were blamed for many of the sufferings of the civilian population during the Emergency. In his novel *Ordeal in the Forest*, Godwin Wachira for example mentions the enormous trench the people of Nyeri and Embu districts had to dig in 1954 in order to make it impossible for the Mount Kenya Mau Mau Army to penetrate the Kikuyu Reserves. 'There were two purposes to this trench: One was to keep the people fully occupied and under close guard so that they could not take into the forest, with the desired effect of making their hatred, resentment and discontent direct itself at the forest fighters rather than towards the white man; and the second was to keep the fighters hemmed in the forest... These people were being treated like slaves and they blamed the forest fighters for each day of slavery that they suffered.'[55] No wonder then that when Mrefu, one of Wachira's forest fighter generals, comes to this trench in order to surrender, he is almost lynched by the angry crowd working on it.

A recent article on General Stanley Mathenge, the lost freedom fighter who is said to be living somewhere in Ethiopia or the Sudan, indicates that even today, some ex-Mau Mau fighters may still be afraid of being blamed for what happened during the Emergency. Asked for the reasons why Mathenge does not return, one of his alleged 'emissaries' is indeed reported to have said: 'We fear our old enemies. Those people we left behind here may turn against us, *making us the scape-goats for the lives lost.*'[56]

Many of the Kikuyu may have found it hard to swallow these bad relations and feelings, and it is quite possible that the image of Mau Mau in the Kikuyu villages is still tarnished by these factors. For the non-fighting population, the memory of Mau Mau certainly revives the sufferings of the Emergency which they blame on the stubborness of the freedom fighters. At the same time they might be ashamed at their betrayal and forsaking of the Mau Mau at a time when the freedom fighters needed help most. This situation also had a very demoralizing effect on the freedom fighters because, 'it left them feeling that they had been cheated; that they had wasted the best years of their lives for a lost cause. If all they had held sacred and dear had become common currency, and even had been turned against them, why need they have suffered at all.'[57] They too then, have some reasons for bitterness and embarrassment in remembering Mau Mau.

Mau Mau as a lost war

Perhaps, the facts we just mentioned would not have had a negative influence on the myth of Mau Mau, if Mau Mau had won the war. This however, has not been the case. In 1956 the revolt 'petered out with no clear results, and its full effects only appeared later', as O. W. Furley said.[58] This statement is in fact watered down somewhat and I think that H. Ruthenberg is nearer to the truth when he claims that 'the effects of the Emergency can, in some respects, be compared to those of a lost war',[59] and that 'when the Emergency ended a long time of assured British rule seemed to lie ahead'.[60] This seems indeed one of the most decisive facts when it comes to analyzing the myth of Mau Mau in the popular tradition: For at least five or six years, from the end of 1954 till the end of 1960, the Kikuyu have not only lived with the idea that they had lost a battle, but that they had lost the war, and that the colonial system was now entrenched more solidly than ever before. The bitterness in

Kikuyu land must have been immense during this period. 'What a misbegotten and worthless dream it all was,' exclaims Mrefu, one of Godwin Wachira's forest fighters, just before surrendering to the security forces,[61] and many freedom fighters must have agreed with him.

Many Kikuyu were probably hit so much harder because they had set high hopes on Mau Mau at the beginning of the Emergency, and because they had sincerely thought that Mau Mau, and Jomo Kenyatta in his Kapenguria trial, were going towards an easy and swift victory: 'Gikonyo walked towards detention with a brisk step and an assurance born in his knowledge of love and life. This thing would end soon, anyway. Jomo would win the case, his lawyers having come all the way from the land of the white man and Gandhi's India. The day of deliverance was near at hand. Gikonyo would come back and take up the thread of life, but this time in a land of glory and plenty.'[62]

The same Gikonyo, in Ngugi's novel *A Grain of Wheat*, comes back from detention six years instead of a few months later, and instead of coming home to a land of glory and plenty, he finds his wife feeding the child of another man, and the Home Guards and the District Officers ruling his village and the whole country as firmly as in 1952. The trial of Kenyatta, also, had definitively been lost.

The accumulated frustrations of the thousands of Gikonyo's in the Kikuyu villages must have coloured the memory of Mau Mau and probably still influence the myth of Mau Mau today. It would be interesting to know what would have happened if Mau Mau had won the war, and if Independence had followed shortly after the Emergency. A comparison between Kenya and Algeria, where Independence indeed coincided with the end of the war, might be very revealing here. I have not studied the case of Algeria sufficiently well to be able to make this comparison, but it seems to me that there has been at least a very important difference between the way Uhuru was celebrated in Kenya and the way Algeria 'danced' its independence.[63] I have in fact got the impression from the description given by Jacques Berque and from the descriptions of people who were in Algeria during the summer of 1962, that for some months a climate of excessive enthusiasm, an atmosphere of real fiesta, completely swept through the whole country. In Kenya, on the other hand, the Uhuru celebrations were much more sober and much more restrained, if not entirely so.

James Ngugi, in *A Grain of Wheat*, probably gives a very good description of the anti-climactic Uhuru celebrations in many villages. When Mugo, the presumed hero, has openly accused himself of betraying Kihika, a moral and emotional shower suddenly seems to have come over the crowd: 'People sat on with bowed heads for a minute or so after Mugo... had gone. Then they rose and started talking, moving away in different directions, as if the meeting ended with Mugo's confession. The sun had faded; clouds were gathering in the sky. Nyamu, Warui, General R. and a few others remained behind to complete the sacrifice before the storm.'[64]

And when Warui, the elder who has fought for freedom since the early days of Harry Thuku in 1922, a few days later recalls Uhuru-day, his meditations are clouded with regret and disappointment: 'Something went wrong... Everybody gone. And a minute before, the field was covered with so many people... Then in the twitching of an eyelid, all gone. The field was so empty. Only four (or were we five?) left. We slaughtered the rams – and prayed for our village. But it was like warm water in the mouth of a thirsty man. It was not what I had waited for, these many years.'[65]

The time lag between the end of the struggle and Independence has been too great, and it seems to me that for this reason *the popular tradition in Kikuyuland will in future remember the Emergency, rather than Mau Mau*, which is of course, a very important difference. Several times I have heard people say: these were hard times, when speaking about the Emergency, but rarely: these were heroic times. This means that the collective Kikuyu memory remembers the hardships and the sufferings during the Emergency period rather than the battles in the forest. Maybe, if Mau Mau had been victorious, it would have been easier to forget the human misery and the lives lost, and to retain first of all, the memories of heroic struggles, as seems to have been the case in Algeria.

This in any case is my hypothesis, although I know that I have only presented one side of the picture. I am aware of the existence of popular songs in Kikuyu praising Mau Mau and extolling the courage and the deeds of the freedom fighters. *Kirima Gia Tumu Tumu* (Tumu Tumu Hill) by Maranga wa Gatonye is one of the examples I have heard of, and there are probably more of these songs. As I did not have the opportunity to make a complete inventory of them and as I only have a rudimentary translation of one of them, I can only express the hope that soon a Kikuyu historian will take up this very interesting theme.

Addendum

While reading the proofs of this book, I found the following item in the *Sunday Nation*, February 18, 1973:

'Over at the National Theatre, Kenneth Watene proves to be probably the first Kenyan dramatist to handle the subject of the independence struggle without velvet gloves.

For his play, *My Son For My Freedom*, is not merely a monument to the cause but debates the effects it had on family and community... Watene sets his story in a small Kikuyu community and through the elderly Gaceru reveals the mental conflict involved in opting for bloodshed; the mental agony of giving orders likely to condemn one's own son...

Through the Mau Mau leader, the author puts the case for violence and internal bloodshed when absolute unity spells the difference between death or survival.'

This sounds very much like resistance literature, but, unfortunately, I have not yet been able to obtain a copy of Mr. Watene's play.

4 The Freedom Fighters

'Strange things happen when the warriors return, and come to the back alley.'[1]

A. Are the freedom fighters neglected?

In October 1971 the following motion was moved in Parliament by the Hon. Waruru Kanja, M.P. for Nyeri:

'That in view of the invaluable role played by the freedom fighters in extricating this nation from the yoke of colonialism and further noting that most of these emancipators lost their property and consequently they or their families are now living in total misery, this House unreservedly records its indebtedness to the liberation movement and resolves to appoint a Select Committee on the Mau Mau war to: –

(a) determine and recommend what financial assistance or otherwise should be given to the freedom fighters who were maimed during the struggle for Independence; and

(b) ascertain the genuineness and extent of the claims of those whose land was confiscated by the colonial regime on account of their involvement in the war with a view to providing needy and deserving cases with pieces of land or compensating them in lieu thereof.'[2]

The motion was strongly opposed by Government spokesmen and ultimately defeated. It was not the first time, and it will probably not be the last either, that the problem of the rewards for the Mau Mau freedom fighters was brought up in Parliament on the initiative of the back-benchers. Already in March 1967, a similar motion was moved, this time by Mr. J. Nthula (KPU, Iveti South), which was later passed by the House. It read:

'In view of the fact that many people who fought and struggled for the independence of this country have been forgotten, and in view of the allegation that these national heroes are often discriminated against by some of their enemies (those who collaborated with the Colonial Government) who are still holding positions of responsibility in this present Government, this House urges the Government to continue to provide, where necessary, land, jobs and educational opportunities for all those who contributed effectively to the freedom struggle.'[3]

Other motions were brought before the House in April 1965 and in June 1969.[4] The first one, moved by Senator R. N. Gikunyu, and asking Government to state as its official policy 'that it recognised the position of the freedom fighters and would do all it could to assist them', was even accepted by the Government.[5]

These facts suggest that the official Government policy in this matter is probably far from satisfactory for the freedom fighters, unless we have to assume that they are completely unreasonable people who never get tired of asking for undeserved Government help. Quite clearly however, while on the one hand the demands of the movers of the different motions become more modest and more limited as time goes on, the attitude of the Government on the other seems to harden. In view of these facts, it becomes interesting to investigate this problem more thoroughly and see if the freedom fighters indeed have some justification for feeling neglected.

Freedom fighters versus Loyalists

Before we can start analyzing factually and in detail what has actually been done for the freedom fighters, a few factors which have or may have been of influence on their material position, must be mentioned here.

First of all, we have to keep in mind that *Mau Mau lost the war*, or more precisely, that in 1956 it seemed that Mau Mau had lost the war. Up till 1962, the Mau Mau fighters emerging from the forest and the detainees released from prison, came back to a society ruled by a colonial administration which they had fought desperately and mercilessly, a colonial administration manned by civil servants and backed by European settlers, the vast majority of whom hated them not only as their actual enemies (in some cases

114

enemies are respected by the British as with Rommel's tank-batallions in the North-African desert battles), but also regarded them as the incarnation of all evil and backwardness. Of course, one could not expect this administration to exert itself for the material welfare of the ex-freedom fighters, and even less to give them preferential treatment. This means that from the end of the actual fighting up till at least 1962, the ex-Mau Mau, more often than not, were going through lean times.

Moreover, the war was not only lost by Mau Mau, it was at the same time won by the Loyalists who, as Home Guards, Government Chiefs and Tribal Policemen, had helped the Kenya administration and the British armed forces to defeat Mau Mau. Of course, these Loyalists were frequently rewarded for their services, many of them getting the opportunity to start a career in the administration or to obtain land and other material advantages in ways that were not always entirely legal or honest.

The important point is that, according to many ex-Freedom Fighters and also quite a few independent observers, this situation did not change much after Independence. These people claim that in 1963, the Loyalists were tacitly allowed to keep the advantages they had reaped under the colonial administration, and that they were quite successful afterwards in holding down the ex-Mau Mau forest fighters and detainees. Even General China, who is certainly not very critical of the actual ruling elite in Kenya, and who is a staunch and loyal supporter of President Kenyatta, states in his Memoirs, published in 1967, that the Kenya Government, at Independence, inherited from the colonial administration the policy of neglecting the freedom fighters.[6] He pleads in very respectful, but at the same time very plain terms, the cause of his less well-off comrades. He also scorns 'some of those who now enjoy the fruits of Independence, who sit in places made available to them partly through the blood and sweat of those who fought', accusing them that they 'look down upon the fighters as fools... and give them no opportunity at all to come up, to regain what they sacrificed'.[7]

Although it is difficult to say who actually 'rules' Kenya today, I can at least quite confidently say that the ex-Freedom Fighters certainly do not rule the roost. As for the Loyalists, it is certain that some of them or their sons, still occupy very high positions in the Kenya Administration and that there has never been any anti-

Loyalist 'witch-hunt' in Kenya. It is also quite characteristic that Kiambu District, which contributed less to the actual Mau Mau fight during the Emergency than all the other Kikuyu Districts, is now over represented in the Kenya Cabinet and probably also at higher administrative levels.[8]

In all probability, therefore, the rewards of the Mau Mau fighters fell far short of their actual expectations. Moreover, they are still partly suffering from the effects of the socio-political situation that was created at the end of their 'lost' war.

A general Kikuyu boom

A second point worth remembering in assessing the problem of the rewards of the freedom fighters is that Kenya has witnessed during the last ten years a general Kikuyu boom. We have seen in the first chapter of this book that the Kikuyu are actually the most advanced and developed group in Kenya and that many people think – sometimes not without proof – that they are favoured as a group by the actual Government.

There can be no doubt that this situation has not only been beneficial to the educated Kikuyu and the city-dwellers, but also to those people who are still living in the Reserves. Most of the money that was spent as part of the Swynnerton Plan between 1954 and 1960 (estimated at a total of £ 10.800.000), flowed into the Kikuyu Reserves,[9] and although the Plan has not been a success all round, it certainly did lead to an increase in agricultural productivity. 'There is little doubt', says D.R.F. Taylor, 'that the Swynnerton Plan initiated an agricultural revolution in Kikuyu land and brought about a great increase in the wealth and the standard of living of the people. Studies in Fort Hall District... have revealed increases of up to 2.000 per cent in monetary income.'[10] H. Ruthenberg, in turn, gives some indications of increased wealth in Nyeri District during the first half of the 1960s, one of them being a rise in marketed agricultural produce from £ 241.000 in 1959 to £ 633.000 in 1964.[11]

Naturally, these facts have to be taken into consideration in this context. Even if the Freedom Fighters have not been rewarded *as Freedom Fighters*, many of them must have benefitted from this general Kikuyu boom *as members of their tribe*. And even if this evolution has mostly been beneficial to the Loyalists, as it is some-

116

times averred, the ex-Freedom Fighters must at least have picked up some of the crumbs that have fallen from the loaded Kikuyu table.[12]

B. What was done for the Freedom Fighters?

In order to find out what the Freedom Fighters actually wanted as rewards for their contribution towards Kenya's Independence, we shall call upon one from their ranks, General China, who in his Memoirs says:

'While the former Freedom Fighters do not seek big jobs for which they may not be qualified, they at least deserve free land on which to maintain themselves – this is what they fought for. Their widows should be aided, and their children given free education. Many of those who were detained lost their land rights... – they should be compensated for this. Those who lost their property ... should also come under a plan for compensation. Similarly, those who were disabled should be housed by the Government, and provided with whatever employment they can manage in the face of their particular handicaps. The graves of those who gave their lives for *Uhuru* are scattered throughout the country... As a gesture of appreciation, and where it is possible, these graves should be located and clearly marked, with memorials to those who lie there. The Government might also establish some form of award for those who distinguish themselves in the service of the country – past, present and future.'[13]

Medals and honours

In analyzing Kenya's policy towards the Freedom Fighters, we shall start at the bottom of General China's list, and deal first with the question of the non-material rewards given to the Freedom Fighters. We have already seen, in the second chapter of this book, that many Forest Fighters were themselves very pre-occupied with the question of how Mau Mau should be commemorated later on. We concluded that the Kenya Government actually seems reluctant to make available any govenment funds for the construction of Mau Mau Memorials, yet at the same time allows, and sometimes even encourages, local initiatives in this domain.

There is also the point of the recognition, not of the Mau Mau revolt as a whole, but of the individual Freedom Fighters and their leaders. This too is a matter which is very close to the hearts of ex-Mau Mau members, as is clear for example from the fact that, in October 1970, some of them intended petitioning President Kenyatta to issue them with special badges. 'We want such badges so that *wananchi* will be able to recognise us', one of them declared on this occasion to a *Daily Nation* reporter.[14] Much earlier, in June 1966, one of the Members of the Senate, Mr. K. Munyi (Embu), had already called upon the Government to award 'liberation medals' to outstanding freedom fighters.[15]

In this matter, however, the Kenya Government has been rather parsimonious. The only Forest Fighter who, to my knowledge, has ever been given an award is General China himself, when in January 1968, he was distinguished with the Order of the Burning Spear (2nd Class), one of Kenya's highest distinctions, although not *the* highest. This distinction was clearly seen by the Government as a kind of collective award for the whole Mau Mau Land Freedom Army as is shown in Mr. Itote's citation which reads: 'A prominent fighter who along with other leading freedom fighters suffered untold miseries in their struggle for Kenya's independence.'[16] Of this citation, which rather clumsily slips from the singular into the plural, one might say that it is poor grammar, but sound politics, in so far that it means at least some sort of recognition of the role of the Forest Fighters in Kenya's history. Up till now, no other Forest Fighter has been honoured by the Government. Moreover, as far as I know, President Kenyatta ignored the demands of the ex-warriors to issue them with badges or other distinctive insignias.

Land confiscated

Some of the most pressing demands of the Freedom Fighters are related to land, one of these being the restitution of the land that was confiscated from Mau Mau members during the Emergency. As is shown by Mr. Kanja's parliamentary motion quoted at the beginning of this chapter, this problem has not yet been resolved to the satisfaction of the freedom fighters, and it is almost certain that the Kenya Government has employed, and is still employing, delaying tactics.

I can hardly find a more apt term to describe the following state-

118

ment by Mr. T. N. Malinda, an Assistant Minister for Lands and Settlement, in answer to a question in Parliament about this problem. Mr. Malinda is reported to have said that 'the total number of acreage of land confiscated during the emergency and the number of families affected, was not readily available. To give such information would require months and months of investigation with other Government departments.'[17]

This is an outright example of playing hide and seek, and is moreover plainly a departure from the official standpoint in September 1964 as stated by Mr. Kenyatta himself: 'Any land that was confiscated during the Emergency has been recorded in the Land Office. Those who had their land taken away will eventually get it back – but this cannot happen overnight.'[18]

From this statement, it is clear that the technical difficulties are probably much smaller than was asserted by Mr. Malinda. The Minister need only consult Mr. Sorrenson's book on land reform which gives some very accurate figures:

'On the 11 July [1955] Native Land Rights Confiscation Orders were issued against seventy-three persons from Kiambu district, ninety-nine from Fort Hall, 113 from Nyeri and thirty-nine in Embu. A week later confiscation orders were issued against a further 333 persons from Kiambu district, 769 from Fort Hall, 1.587 from Nyeri and 408 from Embu. No further orders were issued during the remainder of the year and in 1956 only eleven were issued for Kiambu, seventy-three for Nyeri, five for Embu and not at all for Fort Hall.'[19]

Before July 1955, only 23 Kenyans had had their land confiscated for their real or alleged participation in the Mau Mau movement; they included Kenyatta and some important guerilla leaders like Dedan Kimathi and Stanley Mathenge.[20] The total number of Kenyans against whom confiscation orders were issued is thus 3.533, slightly more than half of them being from Nyeri district. Although Sorrenson admits that it is difficult to estimate how much land was actually confiscated, some persons on the lists (probably between one quarter and one half of them) being landless,[21] these figures would seem to offer quite a reliable working basis for any administration that was really determined to settle the problem and set right the injustices done to the freedom fighters during the Emergency.

Related to the problem of the confiscated lands, is that of the land lost by freedom fighters during the process of land consolidation, which was carried out in Kikuyuland between 1955 and 1960 as part of the Swynnerton Plan. Many Kenyans are still convinced that this whole process of land consolidation has been greatly to the disadvantage of the forest fighters and the detainees. Oginga Odinga, for example, writes in his Memoirs:

'Treachery was well rewarded. The government used the Emergency years to force land consolidation in the Kikuyu reserves. With one and the same reallocation of land holdings the government bought collaborators and wreaked vengeance on the leaders and patriots who were fighting in the forest or detained in the camps... The men in the prisons and detention camps were unable to present their cases before the land consolidation committees. These committees were composed of loyalists and home guards who were bitter enemies of the detainees and took advantage of their absence ... Those who had sacrificed most in the struggle had lost out to people who had played safe.'[22]

It is difficult to say exactly in how far Odinga's accusations are based on fact. In any case, it is interesting to note that some Loyalists pretend that a reverse situation obtained. E. Huxley for example reports a conversation she had with Chief Njiri, an outstanding loyalist, who told her: 'There is too much bribery among the staff, among recorders and measurers. And this bribery goes against the loyalists; they resisted Mau Mau and now, in many cases, the Mau Mau have taken some of their land.'[23] Although Mrs. Huxley herself hesitates to back Chief Njiri's viewpoint,[24] the fact that both parties in the conflict seem to think that their interests have been prejudiced is indicative of the intricacies surrounding the whole problem.

The only person who has published serious research findings on land consolidation in Kikuyuland is Mr. Sorrenson, and I therefore refer readers who require a more complete picture of this issue to his book. Here I will only quote his principal conclusions. On land consolidation in general, Mr. Sorrenson remarks that:

'Despite the early emphasis on using consolidation as a reward for the loyalists, this was not to be consciously pursued to the extent of rewarding them with the land of Mau Mau supporters... Indirectly the loyalists did profit from the confiscation as this land was put into the pool for common land... They have had some influence over the adjudication committees, particularly in the early stages, but this point should not be exaggerated... According to one report, many of the committees at Kiambu were dominated by Mau Mau supporters and, on the whole, they were fairer at adjudication than the loyalists.'[25]

However, there have been important regional differences in land consolidation. In Fort Hall district, so many irregularities were discovered, and so many accusations were slung against the loyalists who had dominated the land committees, that the whole process of consolidation finally had to be done over again in 1961, with the result that in the end there will probably be no 'legacy of unsettled grievances' in this district.[26]

In Kiambu, however, where 'heavy-handed, if at the time efficient, methods'[27] were applied, the Land Office, as late as December 1959, was receiving 700 letters of complaint a month, and the complaints which are left over fill a whole room.[28] Nevertheless Sorrenson has 'little doubt that the majority of Kikuyu accept what has happened; perhaps the only benefit of consolidation and registration that they will acknowledge without qualification is that it stopped expensive litigation.'[29]

It is probably for this reason that the Kenya Government has accepted this particular legacy of the colonial period, and that it has never shown any intention to retract what was done in this field. It must be said that, to my knowledge, no Mau Mau spokesman or political leader has ever asked for such a fundamental measure, which indeed would mean an 'agonizing reappraisal' in the full sense of the term. All that men like Odinga and Kaggia did was to ask for the rectification of particular injustices.

One injustice the Kenya Government is apparently now ready to set right is that of the Emergency villages. During the Emergency the Kikuyu, the Embu and some of the Meru tribesmen were concentrated in 732 villages.[30] At the end of the Emergency, all land owners were gradually allowed to return and live on their land, but many landless persons, among them probably some ex-Mau Mau members who had lost their land, were forced to stay in the villages. On several occasions this matter has been brought up in Parliament, members asking the government to grant land to these people. Recently Mr. J. Angaine, the Minister for Lands and

Settlement, finally announced the intention of the government to find a positive solution to this problem: 'It is also a matter for serious action that eight years after Uhuru, some of our people are still living in Emergency villages. Such people, provided they are genuinely landless and unable to get any job, will be settled by the Government.'[31]

Of course, this measure will not favour ex-Mau Mau members only, for in all probability, some of the inhabitants of the Emergency villages are even former Home Guards, but it will certainly be seen by the freedom fighters as a measure in their favour.

Land given

In the foregoing pages we have dealt with the redressing of injustices rather than with the granting of rewards. Rewards in this field would mean giving free land to the forest fighters, which was one of the things they fought for. It is in fact quite clear from testimonies like Karari Njama's Memoirs that the Forest Fighters, while generally well aware of the fact that they lacked the educational qualifications necessary for top positions in independent Kenya, had nevertheless hoped for some compensation by the new government in the form of farms, as the British Government had done for some of its soldiers after the first and second world war.

The answer to the question of what the new Kenya Government has really done for the forest fighters, however, shows that the dreams of the Mau Mau warriors failed to materialize. During the first three years of Independence, a total of 436 plots were given to former freedom fighters on settlement schemes in the ex-White Highlands,[32] and amongst them were some important leaders of he forest armed forces like Field-Marshal Kimbo, Mr. Kariuki Chetora, Mr. Njoka, General Kamwamba, Mr. James Munene, Mr. Kihoro, General Mwariama and Field-Marshal Salim.[33] Later on, a few more forest fighters seem to have been included in the settlement schemes because in 1971, an official spokesman of the Ministry for Lands and Settlement declared in Parliament that some 600 ex-generals had been settled in Nyandarua District.[34]

This is negligible if one first takes into consideration that, about 85,000 persons were detained in Kenya during the Emergency for their real or alleged participation in Mau Mau, secondly that more than 35,000 families were included in the settlement schemes all over Kenya according to the 1970 report from the Department of Lands and Settlement,[35] and thirdly that the 600 freedom fighters who were chosen for resettlement did not get their land free, but were asked to pay for it on the same conditions as the other African peasants who benefitted from the settlement schemes. On the other hand, it can be taken for granted that, the total of 35,000 families resettled includes a certain number of ex-Freedom Fighters, selected not in their capacity as ex-Mau Mau heroes, but as members of the Kikuyu tribe to whom 40% of the plots in the settlement areas were allotted.

It has been suggested that, especially during the first few months of Independence, many of the ex-Forest Fighters who were offered farms, refused to take up their plots because they did not want to become farmers again.[36] Maybe this was true of some of these warriors who only left the forest at the end of 1963 and who, shortly afterwards, relapsed into rebellion again because they were dissatisfied with the general situation in independent Kenya. They probably formed only a very small minority, because Mr. Angaine, the Minister of Lands and Settlement, declared in an official statement in Parliament in 1966 that 'very few freedom fighters have indeed refused to accept the plots offered to them'. In the same statement he also said that 'in fact the Government has gone out of its way to help freedom fighters who were in real difficulty'[37], which is rather doubtful. The Kenya Government, indeed, went out of its way to give land to the landless all over Kenya, particularly through the one million acre scheme, but it did nothing very special for ex-Mau Mau members.

For a fair picture of the actual position of the freedom fighters we also would have to include in the total number of those who obtained land after Independence, those detainees who remained as free men on the agricultural schemes they had helped to start as forced labourers during the Emergency. This has happened for example on the once notorious Hola irrigation scheme, where, according to an informant from the Ministry of Agriculture, in a total of 295 tenants, 31 Kikuyu farmers were still working in June 1969. According to an article in the *Sunday Nation* this scheme was flourishing at the end of 1971 and four thousand applicants were on the waiting list for admission.[38]

On the Mwea Irrigation Settlement, there are still about 600 ex-detainees holding rice-plots in a total of 2,000 tenants.[39] This is only a very small number compared to the total of 15,000 persons who were detained at Mwea, but at least it can be said that those who were able to stay, today belong to a privileged group in Kenya. President Kenyatta himself referred to the rice scheme at Mwea Tebere as 'a model of its kind, which has attracted much attention within and beyond Africa,'[40] and as far as I know the scheme is indeed generally considered as the prototype of a successful African development project. In 1971 the average net income per tenant from rice crops only, amounted to Shs 2.800,— annually which is between 5 to 6 times more than the national income per family in Kenya; it must be taken into account also that most of the Mwea Tebere tenants have some additional sources of income.[41]

Jobs and army commissions

In an underdeveloped economy where hidden or overt unemployment is rampant, as is the case in Kenya, any group asking for special favours will give a high priority to preferential treatment in the field of employment. The ex-freedom fighters have not been an exception to this rule. Up till now, they have been very unsuccessful in this campaign, the policy of the Government having been remarkably and consistently negative, except in one respect.

This exception is the reinstatement with full privileges of those Kenyans who lost their job through their Mau Mau activities during the Emergency. As far as I know, this issue has been satisfactorily resolved and very little is heard of it nowadays. But even this seems not to have had an entirely smooth and easy passage. In October 1965, Bildad Kaggia could still complain in Parliament about this matter, saying that he had 'a list of 400 people who had been attempting to resume jobs with railway administration for many years... As late as August last year, these people were still receiving replies from the railways advising them to obtain a "white certificate" from their District Commissioners.'[42] If one knows that a 'white certificate' was only given to people who had never had any connexion with Mau Mau or were regarded as people who had completely 'confessed' and had been completely 'rehabilitated', one will understand the *raison d'être* behind the motion passed in Parliament calling for the reinstatement of such people.[43]

124

As for preferential treatment in obtaining new jobs, the ex-Mau Mau members have been largely unsuccessful. In May 1971, the issue was brought up in Parliament by Mr. J. Muturia, Member for Nyambene North, who received a very forthright and negative reply from the Minister of Labour. 'Every Kenya national who registers as a job seeker is advised to get employment in what part of the Republic it is available and no special cards are issued to former freedom fighters who register for jobs... In the eyes of the Ministry all jobseekers were regarded as Individuals, whether they were freedom fighters, forest fighters, etc.'[44] It was on this occasion that Mr. W. Kanja, ex-Mau Mau detainee and Member for Nyeri, was forced to withdraw some remarks he made to the address of the Minister to the effect that he had done nothing in the struggle for Uhuru, while the Mau Mau were fighting.[45]

One possible way of giving preferential treatment to the ex-freedom fighters and especially to the forest fighters in the employment sector, would have been to allow them to enroll in the Kenya Armed Forces. Many of them would certainly have liked this, as is reported by Waruhiu Itote (ex-General China), who confirms in his book that, in August 1963, 'people still in the forest had requested permission to form their own battalion in the new Kenya Army, and wanted their own tents, uniforms, and mess hall'.[46] From this time onwards, several Kenya politicians have proposed such a solution. They range from Mr. Fred Kubai, now an Assistant Minister in the Kenya Government, who, in July 1963, suggested that former Mau Mau 'generals' and their followers should be recruited to form an 'army of liberation' to be used against South Africa and other 'Fascist States',[47] to Mr James Njiru, M.P. for Kirinyaga West, who, in September 1971, told Parliament that Kenya's Armed Forces should be given guerrilla training with the help of former forest fighters.[48] In between, other politicians suggested that the Mau Mau fighters should be engaged against the Somali *shifta*,[49] or sent to help the Congolese rebels in 1964–65.[50]

The Kenya Government, however, has never reacted positively to statements and requests of this nature, partly because of the limited usefulness of the forest fighters for the purposes of modern, regular warfare. But it is probably nearer the truth to say that the forest fighters who wanted to enlist were willing to do so on terms that differed too much from those of the Government. First of all, as we have seen, some of them wanted their own regiments and uniforms, but, as General China pointed out in his Memoirs, it was practically impossible for the Kenyatta Government to concede this point at the risk of incurring 'charges of "Mau Mauism" had these people been absorbed wholesale into the army.'[51] Secondly, some Mau Mau Generals and Field-Marshals, when half-seriously invited to enlist in the Kenya Rifles at the beginning ranks.[52]

The few forest fighters, who finally managed to enroll in the Kenya Army did indeed 'loose their ranks'. General China himself, once one of the three most outstanding military leaders of the Mau Mau forces, had to enlist as a private, after his release from detention in 1962. He was forced to undergo a severe, and sometimes very humiliating training, supervised by some of the very same British officers he had once fought, before he eventually became an officer and later on, Deputy Director of the Kenya Youth Service. According to China's information, a few more former Forest Fighters were nominated as Officer Trainees at the same time as he himself was nominated,[53] but their number was insignificant compared to the number of people who had had some experience as forest fighters during the Emergency.

The fact that the Kenya Government has never encouraged a massive enrolment of ex-Mau Mau warriors in the Army, is all the more surprising when viewed against the increasingly enforced Kikuyuisation of this same Army which has been going on for some years. It is probably symptomatic of the fundamental mistrust in which the freedom fighters are held by the Government and it would be interesting to know why they are so mistrusted: for their military and technical incapacities, or for their lack of political loyalty? Probably the two factors play a role.

Allowances and education

Three categories would seem to qualify for eventual government allowances as a compensation for losses endured because of the Emergency: The disabled and maimed, the widows, and the orphans. The Kenya Government has no consistent policy towards any of these three categories and did, or has done, nothing for them. As far as the disabled freedom fighters are concerned we can refer readers to Mr. Kanja's defeated parliamentary motion of

October 1971 which especially mentioned this category as one of the two urgent issues on the list of injustices to be redressed[54] and also to Leonard Kibera who, in his book *Voices in the Dark* and in his short story *1954*, strongly takes sides with those 'who got shot before they could free their country and now have to beg money from those who shot them.'[55]

The 'widows of the Emergency' seem to be very much in the same position as the disabled, that is to say, they are generally neglected to the point of near oblivion. Some facts lead us to believe that the needs of many of them must be great. In March 1968, for example, Mr. Angaine, the Minister for Lands and Settlement, on a tour of the Northern part of his Meru homedistrict, donated sums of 300 sh. to the widows of the Emergency in several villages.[56] This certainly speaks for the generosity and the social conscience of the Minister, but it is at the same time a strong indication of the absence of any serious government policy in this matter. As late as October 1970, another Government Minister, Mr. Paul Ngei, said in a speech in Nairobi that the widows of the freedom fighters should be assisted by the authorities, and that this should not be considered a privilege because they 'gave all they had for the cause of independence'.[57] One of his suggestions was to provide them with land, which indeed happened in the case of a few like Mrs. Dedan Kimathi and Mrs. Stanley Mathenge, who are included in the number of about 600 freedom fighters who were given farms in the new settlement areas.

For the orphans of the emergency, the situation seems slightly better, but only very slightly, and the difference might be more apparent than real. Already in 1965, Bildad Kaggia made himself one of their spokesmen inside and outside Parliament.[58] In all probability, not much was done for them at that time, because the matter came up again in Parliament at the beginning of October 1970 when a question about the general compensation of the families of former freedom fighters was answered by Mr. Munyi, an Assistant Minister in the Office of the President. After he had stated that the Government 'could not entertain the question of compensating thousands of people who fought for the country's independence,'[59] the Assistant Minister added as a positive point that Dedan Kimathi's children were getting bursaries from the Government, which was promptly denied by Mr. J. K. Muregi,

Member for Nyandarua South, the constituency where Mrs. Kimathi lives.

For once, the Government and President Kenyatta acted quickly on a Mau Mau issue. Less than two weeks later, in his Kenyatta Day speech, Kenya's first citizen was greeted with 'prolonged cheers' when he said: 'Some of our gallant freedom fighters left children behind them, and the best tribute we can pay to the memory of these brave men is to ensure that their children are given training to help them find a place in our new Kenya.'[60] As a practical measure, Mr. Kenyatta announced in his speech that he had instructed the Provincial Commissioners of Kenya's seven provinces and Nairobi to select 15 boys and 5 girls each between the ages of 16 and 22, and orphans of the Emergency, in order to send them to the National Youth Service for care and training.

Thus at least something was done, but before we conclude on this optimistic note, this 'generous and magnanimous gesture'[61] of Mr. Kenyatta deserves a few remarks. First of all a total of 160 boys and girls to be educated by Government seems rather small if one recalls that at least 11,500 Mau Mau fighters perished between 1952 and the end of 1956 alone.[62] Secondly, the Government authorities have waited rather long before deciding to care for and train children, some of whom must have been orphans for already 18 years. It is true that, at the age of 16 to 22, one can still give some help to an unemployed and ill-trained adolescent, but in trying to give a real education to the orphans of the Emergency, Mr. Kenyatta's gesture came years too late. Finally, one wonders why all the seven provinces of Kenya were asked to select a similar number of destitute children. It is no secret that the Mau Mau war was mostly fought out in the Kikuyu areas of Central Province; in some other provinces, it must have been quite difficult to find the required number of genuine Emergency orphans. The editorial writer of the *Daily Nation*, however, found it 'gratifiying to note that ... President Kenaytta has decided to spread the benefit evenly,'[63] and in a way one can understand his point. If it is true that 'we all fought for Uhuru,' as Kenya's official Uhuru myth has it, then quite naturally Mr. Kenyatta was perfectly right in looking for Emergency orphans everywhere in Kenya.

C. Mau Mau pressure groups

Of course, the freedom fighters or part of them, have on several occasions, tried to organize themselves in order to defend their interests – materially and morally. They have done so by forming pressure groups intended to be active in the political arena and by founding economic associations. Other groups, like the Kenya People's Union, and some individuals like J. M. Kariuki, have also tried permanently or intermittently, to act as spokesmen for the freedom fighters. We shall first analyze the actions and failures of these groups before coming to a general evaluation of the Kenya Government's policy towards the ex-freedom fighters.

Political organizations

The first politically minded Mau Mau pressure groups were already founded years before Independence. This was, for example, the case with KKM (Kiama Kia Muingi), an association which probably originated in Kiambu in 1955 and which was revived in 1957–58, particularly in Fort Hall district. The colonial government actively and successfully combatted KKM, presenting it to the outside world as a simple revival of Mau Mau in another form. However, it appears that such an interpretation of the movement was rather biased. According to M.P.K. Sorrenson and especially to J. M. Kariuki, KKM was also, or as the latter affirms even exclusively, a sort of Mau Mau welfare organization, seeking by political means and pressures compensation for the losses suffered by Mau Mau activists and sympathizers during the Emergency, particularly in the field of land consolidation.[64]

It is of course no wonder that the colonial government, as long as it held the reigns of power in Kenya, systematically outlawed any organization which tried to revive Mau Mau, or had even the slightest connexion with the Mau Mau movement. The fact that the Government of independent Kenya consistently tried to do the same is much more unexpected. Yet this is what happened. There is no organization in existence in present day Kenya representing the former freedom fighters and detainees and which acts as a political pressure group on their behalf. The reasons for this however are not clear.

According to General China, who is one of the very few observers who has tried to enter into the merits of this touchy subject, the ex-Mau Mau members are, themselves, largely responsible for the non-existence of a freedom fighters' organization representing their interests. 'In October 1963' General China writes, '... the Government agreed to provide two offices where the forest leaders could sort out their records of those who had been killed or wounded in the struggle, and those who had lost their property. The group could then employ constitutional means to secure compensation ... The plan failed, however, when the fighters found it impossible to agree on who should be their leader and spokesman. They had not yet been able to organize themselves outside the forest, and thus have lost many opportunities for improving their condition.' [65]

I have not been able to find out whether General China's version of these events is true. However, in view of the situation at the end of 1963, and considering the tensions between those who stayed in the forest till Independence, those who surrendered or were captured before, and those who were only detained without having been in the forest, as well as the internal strife between several field-marshals all laying claim to the exclusive leadership of the first group, the difficulties concerning the founding of one overall freedom fighters' organization become understandable. China's thesis was in fact confirmed to me by one of the managers of NDEFFO, an agricultural cooperative society run by ex-Mau Mau members, when I questioned him on the origins of his own organisation.

On the other hand, one also gains the impression that the Kenya Government was far from unhappy about this dissension and used it as a very convenient pretext to lay the blame elsewhere. In fact, as soon as the freedom fighters or part of them, did manage to overcome their quarrels and founded Mau Mau pressure groups of some kind, the Government promptly outlawed these associations. Already in 1963, C. Sanger suggested that before Independence Mr. Kenyatta refused a request of the tens of thousands of ex-detainees to form a welfare association,[66] which is in contradiction to China's version. As I have not been able to verify this, I find it rather difficult to choose between the versions of General China and Mr. Sanger.

About a year later, however, as some news items in the Kenya press indisputably prove, an ex-Freedom Fighters' Association did exist, and this association, the Kenya Freedom Fighters' Union, was indeed refused registration.[67] According to the newspaper reports, this association was mainly operating in Naivasha area, and had as its overall aim to bring together all Kenyans who had been in the forest during the Emergency. More specifically, the aims of the association seemed to be to force the Government to give free land to the forest fighters, to stop Africans from buying land from Europeans and to try and obtain compensation for those who had lost property during the Emergency.[68] Members apparently also took an oath pledging themselves to steal cows from European farms and never to allow their daughters to marry a Home Guard or a member of the security forces.[69]

As this association acted as a secret society binding its members by means of nocturnal oaths, and as some of its aims conflicted entirely with a few of the key-dogmas of official Government policy ('Forgive and forget' would mean that a Kenya girl could marry anybody, even a Home Guard; European land and cattle were not to be taken away, but had to be paid for), one understands the authorities' unequivocal declaration of war on this apparently local Union which was capable of reviving old fears among the European population whom the Government wanted to placate. Nevertheless some of the freedom fighters must have gained the impression from these events that they had still not won the war, and that they were considered a nuisance rather than an asset in official Government circles.

At the beginning of 1969, the Kenya Government, once again, gave proof of its determination not to allow ex-freedom fighters to run any associations that might have direct political overtones. In February of that year, three Mau Mau organisations (The Kenya War Council, the ex-Freedom Fighters' Union and the Walioleta Uhuru Union, which means the Union of Those who Brought Uhuru), were banned by the Attorney General, Mr. Charles Njonjo. Very little was said in the press about the reasons for this measure, except that the societies in question were considered by the Attorney General as 'dangerous to the good government of the Republic'.[70] Yet it is evident that the main reason was that, by their very existence, and in most of their demands, they were in conflict with some of the fundamental dogmas of Kenya politics since the early 1960's. As for the 'Union of Those who Brought Uhuru', it is clear that there is no place for a society of this name in a country where 'we all fought for Uhuru,' because it suggests the existence of a sort of freedom fighters' elite which is denied or ignored by the official ideology. Similar reproaches were probably also made against the other two organizations. I have also been told by a rather well-informed Kenya journalist that the ex-Freedom Fighters' Union which was presided over by Mr. James Njiru, now a Member of Parliament, was also banned because of its frequent requests for 'free things' such as farms and education for the children of Mau Mau fighters. This again conflicted with one of President Kenyatta's urgent slogans: *Uhuru na Kazi* [Freedom and Work.]

The ex-Freedom Fighters are apparently then not allowed to play a part in *Kenya politics*, at least not as a group. They are however, allowed, and maybe even encouraged, to play a role in *Kenya's political folklore*. It happens not infrequently at official celebrations like Kenyatta Day or simply at speeches of President Kenyatta when he tours Central Province or the Rift Valley Province that 'Mau Mau freedom fighters' teams' dressed in tattered clothes, with plaited hair, and carrying *pangas* and 'home-made' wooden guns, turn up to take part in the festivities.[71] A much photographed team of this kind, and one that appears more or less to monopolize this folkloristic function for Nakuru District, is the Nakuru District Ex-Freedom Fighters' Organization (NDEFFO), an organization we shall meet again in the following section of this chapter when dealing with Mau Mau associations of a mainly economic nature.

Economic associations

When they saw the political road was barred to them and recognized the futility of waiting any longer for 'free things', some groups of freedom fighters decided a few years ago to go it alone and work out a solution which characterizes the Kikuyu mentality and the Kikuyu way of living: They started founding economic associations with the aim of buying farms or starting business enterprises. Most of these societies are of the cooperative type, having from a few dozen up to some thousands of members who pay for a share in the company in the hope of reaping benefits once the society is well on its way to success.

132

The most important and the best-known of these societies is NDEFFO, or Nakuru District Ex-Freedom Fighters' Organization Ltd. which, to the best of my knowledge, was first heard of in the beginning of 1968 and which was officially registered as a company in March 1968. The aims of the society can best be described in the words of Mr. Kimunya Kamana, the General Manager and one of the driving forces behind the whole movement. In a speech to NDEFFO members in January 1968, he was reported to have said that 'the Government did not believe in free things and would only help those who helped themselves. Their organization was completely non-political and its main object was to collect money to buy farms for the members. He pointed out that they would not hesitate to help the Government deal with those who worked against the Regulations.'[72]

As is indicated by the name of the society, its founders were ex-freedom fighters, and according to information given to me by a leading member of the company in September 1971, all the members are still either ex-forest fighters or ex-detainees. I was given to understand however that there is no juridical barrier to a non-freedom fighter or even a non-Kikuyu becoming a member of the society, but that other people simply refrain from joining because they are still somewhat afraid of Mau Mau. Even a European like myself could become a NDEFFO-member, my informant assured me, but when I asked what the fee was, I was told there were no membership-places available at that particular moment. I nevertheless got the impression that the leaders of the company are sincere in claiming that they do not want to be an entirely exclusive Mau Mau group, and that they really would accept members from other backgrounds. At the same time, however, they are still very conscious and proud of their Mau Mau past.

Actually NDEFFO owns three farms totalling 7,500 acres, again according to personal information given by one of its directors, and in September 1971, the society was negotiating the purchase of a fourth farm comprising about 3,500 acres. These farms are cultivated and managed as economic units as was the case when they were still owned by European settlers. Some landless and jobless members of the society apparently are allowed to live and work on the farms while at the same time cultivating a small plot for their personal use.

It is rather difficult to get a precise idea about the actual economic and financial position of NDEFFO and about its future prospects. Although I did not visit any of their farms, my own impressions from interviews with the managers were very favourable, and I was assured by people with more knowledge and experience of agronomics than myself that the company is generally considered in Kenya as a dynamic and thriving enterprise with a good future. I have also gained the impression that the Kenya Government is rather favourably disposed towards NDEFFO, and that it would not let the company down in case of financial difficulties, although it does not support the group today. This impression is further strengthened because, not only does NDEFFO appear to have a sort of exclusive right to the freedom-fighters' folklore-performances in the Rift Valley Area, but also because there is good reason to believe that the Government has intervened at least once on behalf of the company, namely when it was negotiating for one of the farms it now owns.

This happened in the spring of 1968 when NDEFFO-members illegally occupied Engoshura Farm, which was then for sale and for which the society had made a bid lower than the total of two other potential buyers who each wanted to purchase part of the farm.[73] It is impossible to know what exactly happened, but it is quite clear that the NDEFFO-leaders felt greatly encouraged in their actions by a discussion they had had with the Minister for Lands and Settlement at the end of March of that year.[74] Moreover it is generally known that subsequently, all other bids on the disputed farm, even those that exceeded NDEFFO's offer, were refused by the Land Board, which apparently divulged no reasons for this. In January 1970, it was suddenly announced that NDEFFO had definitively acquired the ownership of Engoshura Farm, which seems to give strength to the rather strong presumptions of lobbying behind the scenes.

Despite the dynamism of its leaders, however, the financial position of NDEFFO at the end of 1971 was rather precarious. The nominal capital of the society at that moment stood at £ 75.000 (850 Kenya sh. = 50 English pounds). But in 1969 and 1970 the company had suffered heavy losses, totalling about £ 21.500. [75] These losses are probably partly due to incompetence and poor book-keeping, but probably also because NDEFFO is not just a commercial enterprise, but a sort of Mau Mau 'Commune' which tries to take care of its members 'from the cradle to the grave'. I was in fact told that, the company does a lot of social and educational work for its 5500 members, and that several schools and a nursery have been built on the farms owned by NDEFFO. The NDEFFO directors even seem to dream of founding a secondary school on one of their farms, and they also informed me of their intention to concentrate all the orphans of the Emergency on the fourth estate they negotiated for in September 1971, with the aim of offering them educational assistance.[76]

These plans and the extra-economic activities already under-taken, of course require a lot of money and must partly account for the company's losses. It is also probable that NDEFFO members living on the farms consume part of the agricultural produce, which is thus never entered in the accounts. Anyway, the NDEFFO attempt to better the life of the ex-freedom fighters by hard work and commercial enterprise is a very interesting experiment which deserves a much more thorough analysis than I have been able to give it.

NDEFFO is certainly the most dynamic and the most successful of the companies of its kind, but there are some other Mau Mau groups that have refrained from politics and have tried their luck instead in business. One of them is the Kenya Kariba Buro Company Ltd., chaired by the former Mau Mau general Mbaria Kaniu, who was once a leading commander in Kimathi's Aber-dares Army. This Naivasha company suddenly hit the headlines of the Kenya Press in September 1971, when its leaders accused the European managers of two big farms in the neighbourhood of Naivasha, of having illegally evicted some African workers. Sub-sequently they announced their decision to buy these farms despite the fact that they were not for sale and that the company, according to the figures published in the press, was not in a position to raise the money, even if the farms were for sale.[77]

For a few days, this affair was extensively covered by the *Daily Nation*. It was however not followed up and unfortunately I have no information about the final outcome, although I doubt very much whether Kariba Buro will ever be financially strong enough to realize its intentions.

The financial situation of this society seems in fact, not very bright. Regrettably I cannot supply any precise information because in September 1971 the firm's financial report for 1970 had not yet reached the Registrar's Office.

It is also not quite certain to what extent Kariba Buro is really a 'Mau Mau' society as is the case with NDEFFO. In the *Daily Nation* articles, the emphasis was strongly on the Mau Mau aspect of the affair as is clear from the headlines ('No price is too high for farms, say ex-Mau Mau'[78]; 'Ex-Mau Mau lead bid to buy farms'[79]) and the entire text. Mr. Githaki Kariuki (General Kahonoki), an important member of the society, was, for example, reported to have given as one of the reasons why the society wanted to buy one of the two farms that:

'The Masai want to buy the grave of one of our famous and courageous Mau Mau generals... General Lengele ... who was shot by Europeans at the farm when he went to get food. Masai have resolved they must buy the farm.'[80]

When questioned, the leaders of Kariba Buro I have been able to meet, showed some irritation about these press comments, and declared that, although founded by ex-Mau Mau Generals, their society was not at all exclusive, but open to all Kenya citizens. Apparently they felt a need to dissociate themselves from too close a connexion with the freedom fighters.[81]

The battle for the Rift Valley

Despite this wish of its leaders for 'respectability', Kariba Buro is symptomatic of a sort of illogical and quite unreasoned longing one often finds in ex-freedom fighters circles: the urgent and compelling desire to acquire in one way or another the 'promised lands' of the Rift Valley. 'We must get this farm', 'We must buy it'; these were expressions that were used by all the Kariba Buro Directors I met, with almost prophetic tones in their voice. It appears that these ex-Mau Mau Generals, when they organize their followers in order to buy farms in the Rift Valley, in a certain sense are doing nothing very new, but are just trying to implement the old Mau Mau programme of 'freeing the land', this time with means better suited to the circumstances:

'If the President of this country allowed us to snatch these farms we could do so tonight,' Mr. Mbaria Kaniu is reported to have said in September 1971. 'We are under Mzee's Government, which

136

does not believe in snatching other people's property. Land is however ours, and that is why we fought. We want, and we are ready to buy, property on any of these two farms to provide shelter for our people living in villages as squatters.'[82]

Of course this Kikuyu, and in many ways ex-Mau Mau, drive to control the Rift Valley, does not please everybody in Kenya. It is in fact quite clear that, since Independence and already slightly before, a persistent underground battle is going on in Kenya over the question as to who will be able to get hold of that part of the White Higlands which was temporarily left in the hands of the European settlers and where Africans of all ethnic groups can buy land without being restricted by tribal quotas and allotments as in the African settlement areas. While the Kikuyu and the Kalenjin are the most important competitors in this struggle, some minor groups like the Masaï and the Wanderobo also occasionally play a role in the issue. Kenya's political leaders have had the greatest difficulties in keeping these tribal rivalries within the limits of normal economic competition, and time and again Mr. Kenyatta and Vice-President arap Moi were forced to tour the Rift Valley Region in order to preach the virtues of cooperation and tribal harmony. The conflict between the NDEFFO company and other bidders for Engoshura farm also had such a tribal background. The debates in Parliament on this issue in fact reveal that it was feared that the Kalenjin squatters who were working on the farm under European management, would be evicted as soon as the Kikuyu-dominated NDEFFO got hold of it. In this case the debates in Parliament ended on a humorous note when Mr. Oloitiptip took the floor and said that 'it was obviously a tribal squabble between the Kalenjin and Kikuyu, neither of whom even knew the meaning of the word Engoshura. He was not tribally-minded but he should point out that the land belonged to neither the Kikuyu nor the Kalenjin – it was Masaï land.'[83]

Most of the time, however, humour is conspicuously absent in debates of this kind as, for example, in September 1971 when Mr. Mark Mwithaya, M.P. for Nakaru Town, brought before the House the issue of the 10,000 acre Ngata Farm which was the source of a conflict between a Kikuyu group and a society known as Kalenjin Enterprise Co. During this debate Mr. S.K. Kurgat, one of the spokesmen of the Kalenjin Group, declared that: 'The

Kalenjin enterprise was going to buy the Ngata Farm... irrespective of what the cost of the farm was... We are not prepared to withdraw. We have deposited money for the farm. If anybody is prepared to deposit £ 50,000 for the same farm then we will deposit £ 500,000 for it. I am sounding a warning that we are prepared to retaliate if anybody provokes us..'[84]

Land is still an important, if not the most important issue in Kenya today, and it is interesting to see how eager the average Kikuyu is to join enterprises like NDEFFO and Kariba Buro. 'Mau Mau is still alive' declare the NDEFFO posters that are brought to political meetings and other public functions. In a way this is quite true, as we have now seen.

The limits of economic organizations
There are, or have been, also some ex-freedom fighters' groups which went into business rather than try to buy farms. One of them is the Embu District Branch of the 'Kenya Old Comrades Association,' which seems to be composed of 'Second World War ex-army officers who also took part in Kenya's freedom fight'.[85] Some years ago there was also a group of ex-forest fighters who tried to found a publishing house with the intention of giving more publicity to Mau Mau and its struggle for Independence. According to an informant from East Africa Publishing House, this group actually managed to issue a few booklets on Mau Mau written in Kikuyu, but at the end of 1971 they had apparently ceased their activities.[86]

A very interesting case, because it is quite recent and because it shows clearly the limits imposed on Mau Mau associations even today, is the Kenya Old Mau Mau Company, a group which called a meeting in Nairobi on the 5th of September 1971 in order to raise funds to start a business company financed by ex-Mau Mau members.[87] The group apparently managed to raise some money, but very soon the company got into trouble, because on the occasion of the opening of its offices in October 1971, the Provincial Commissioner of Nairobi warned already that 'Mau Mau was a sacred name in Kenya's history and should not be used as a commercial name... He appealed to leaders of the group to change the name of the company.'[88]

On the same occasion the chairman of the group declared that it 'was not political and its main aim was to write books and make films on the Mau Mau movement which fought for Kenya's independence.'[89]

Nothwithstanding a change of name from Old Mau Mau United Company to Old Matigari Enterprise,[90] and the reassurances of its leaders about the non-political character of the association, it was declared dangerous to the good government of the Republic of Kenya and banned in February 1972 by the Attorney General.[91] Two other societies, the Kenya Old Mau Mau Traders, Farmers and Miners Company and the Kenya Ex-Detainees Trading and Farmers Company, were also scrapped from the register. I have no information about the latter, but the first company used the same Post Office Box as the Old Mau Mau United Company and at least one of its directors was on both managing boards. It can thus be assumed that they were more or less identical.

The Registrar of Societies, Mr. D.J. Coward, was not very talkative about the reasons for this measure, but he nevertheless declared to a *Daily Nation* reporter that the associations had been holding meetings, collecting subscriptions and undertaking activities unconnected with their business, which meant that they had tried to evade the strict control of society registration by registering as commercial companies.[92] Put in other terms: they were political organizations in disguise. The following day it was even suggested in the press that, 'certain irresponsible elements in these companies' had tried to 'inject into the consciences of their followers sectarian oaths,'[93] which, if this is true, means that they were a sort of outright revival of the Mau Mau movement.

It appears then that the Kenya Government is extremely vigilant on the issue of Mau Mau, and that it is rather reluctant to give the freedom fighters any 'opportunity at all to come up, to regain what they sacrificed,'[94] unless they keep strictly within the narrow limits of neutral economic activities as does NDEFFO. Even the NDEFFO managers, however, are probably under no illusions as to these limits, because they were warned at least once by the Rift Valley Provincial Commissioner, Mr. Simon Nyachae 'that politics should not be practised in any way by the company. If it did, it could collapse'.[95]

Mau Mau spokesmen: Kaggia and the KPU

In the absence of officially recognised Mau Mau pressure groups, the interests of the freedom fighters are taken care of by a few individual politicians acting more or less on their own initiative. The first to be mentioned here, because his fight has been the most intensive and the most persistent, is Bildad Kaggia, himself an ex-detainee, who was arrested together with Jomo Kenyatta on October 20, 1952 and convicted with him at Kapenguria. Before his arrest, Kaggia had played a key role in the Nairobi Central Committee, which certainly was one of the most radical associations in Kenya in 1951–52, and although he has not been a forest fighter himself, having been already detained before the real fighting broke out, he can be considered as an important Mau Mau leader.

During his detention his radical convictions underwent no change, and when he was finally released in the beginning of the 1960s, he at once started to campaign in favour of Kenya's many dispossessed, of whom the ex-freedom fighters were, in his opinion, part and parcel. Already before Independence, he protested strongly when Kenya's new leaders decided to *buy* European farms instead of just taking them away without compensation and distributing the land freely to the landless. After Independence, he redoubled his attacks, which very soon brought him into open conflict with President (then still Prime-Minister) Kenyatta. In the beginning of the spring of 1964 he was dismissed from his post of Parliamentary Secretary to the Minister of Education, according to his own testimony 'because of his continual attacks on the Ministry of Lands and Settlement' and because 'he had been fighting to have land confiscated from freedom fighters during the Emergency returned to the rightful owners'.[96]

There can be no doubt that it has largely been through the efforts of Kaggia that the defence of the interests of the freedom fighters became an important issue in the political platform of the Kenya People's Union, when this more radical party was founded in 1966. The distribution of free land to 'those who lost their lands in the struggle for independence, either by expropriation or through land consolidation' became thus an official item in the KPU programme although it was also stated that: 'The KPU recognizes that consolidation in areas affected, is now an accomplished fact and it would be indesirable to disturb it. Those who are now owners of consolidated land will be left in undisturbed possession. Compensation will therefore take the form of land acquired from European settlers.'[97]

It is interesting to note that both KANU and the newly founded KPU, in April and May 1966, tried to enroll the freedom fighters in their campaigns, with varying success. Different groups of people, pretending to represent them, indeed issued manifestoes and held meetings during these politically rather feverish months, pledging loyalty to KANU (and Kenyatta) or to KPU (and Odinga), and accusing the other party of using the freedom fighters as 'pawns in their political schemes'.[98] It is of course difficult to say who were more successful in winning the sympathies of the freedom fighters, but the fact that Bildad Kaggia in the subsequent elections in his Kandara constituency was heavily defeated by his KANU opponent, seems to indicate that most of the ex-Mau Mau members remained loyal to President Kenyatta, even if they may have shared some of Kaggia's views on the Government treatment they were receiving. It must also be said that the Government succeeded in enlisting some well-known ex-forest fighters like Field-Marshal Mwariama, General Kimbo and General Mbaria Kaniu, who publicly expressed their confidence in President Kenyatta, while the KPU freedom fighters' manifestoes I have seen were signed by persons unknown to me and probably of lesser importance during the Emergency struggle.

Some former Mau Mau Generals, in these heated days, even declared at an official May Day rally in Nairobi 'that they had been offered £ 150.000 by Mr. Oginga Odinga to revive the cult..., to return to the forests and overthrow the Government,'[99] an offer, they claimed, they had of course rejected, and which, very probably, had never been made at all.

Anyway, during the few years of its existence, KPU regularly brought up, in Parliament and elsewhere, the issue of the rewards of the freedom fighters. Thus it became part and parcel of a general political conception, a conception more egalitarian and 'socialist' than the one inspiring KANU leaders like President Kenyatta and Tom Mboya. It is also interesting that in Parliament, the interests of the freedom fighters were taken care of by KPU MP's of Luo origin, all the Kikuyu candidates like Kaggia having been defeated in the elections. As far as I can judge, these Luo members performed their duty towards the freedom fighters conscientiously and competently, which is a strong argument in favour of the non-tribal, ideological character of their party.

In the mean time, Mr. Kaggia continued to campaign in favour of the ex-Mau Mau members by means of 'extra-parliamentarian' actions, and even when he resigned from KPU in August 1969, he took great pains to make it clear that he only rejoined KANU because KPU had become 'less and less effective', and that he intended to go on with his struggle for the freedom fighters because he wanted to see to it 'that the people of Kenya in general and the children and widows of Dedan Kimathi, Stanley Mathenge and all other Mau Mau heroes will always say that the precious blood of these gallant Kenyans was not shed for nothing'.[100]

Since then, however, Kaggia's role in Kenya politics has been very limited, and his fight for the Mau Mau heroes has been rather discreet up till now. His forthcoming Memoirs will probably prove that he still holds the same opinions and that he has lost nothing of his old vigour and sympathies for those who 'lost out to the people who played safe in our most difficult days'.[101]

Mau Mau spokesmen: KANU Backbenchers
The case of the freedom fighters has not only been advocated in Parliament by Mr. Kaggia and the KPU, but also – and sometimes very explicitly – by some KANU Backbenchers. This was already the case before KPU existed, and it went on even when KPU was represented in Parliament. Today too, there are still some staunch defenders of the Freedom Fighters in Parliament like Mr. J. Muturia (Nyambene North), who asked several questions about Mau Mau issues in June 1971, and Mr. W. Kanja (Nyeri) 'who roars like a lion in Parliament when the subject of Mau Mau fighters comes up and who is never tired of speaking up for the freedom fighters whenever he gets the opportunity'.[102]

A few other parliamentarians are also favourably disposed towards the freedom fighters and highly critical of the Government policy on this matter, which is quite in agreement with Kenya's longstanding tradition of a critical and independent Legislature. However, something has changed since the banning of KPU: Today the case of Mau Mau is brought up as a single issue and no longer as an integral part of a radical, alternative policy for Kenya as a nation. Some MP's even show tendencies to slide back and see it not as a problem at the national level but only at the own constituency level.

In May 1971, for example, Mr. Muturia once again raised the subject of jobs for the freedom fighters in Parliament, but what he sought to know this time was 'how many freedom fighters *from his constituency* had been offered jobs in the Republic'.[103] This means that the defence of the interests of the ex-Mau Mau members tends to become more and more an isolated battle fought by some scattered individuals. The efficiency of their actions will probably suffer from this, which is all the more dangerous as the Kenya Government apparently never gave much attention to the numerous questions raised in Parliament since Independence.

Mau Mau spokesmen: Kariuki and China

Two persons, who both played an important role in the Mau Mau struggle, the first as a detainee-leader in the detention camps, and the second one as a general in the forest, must again be mentioned here for their campaigns to gain recognition for the freedom fighters. The first of them is J.M. Kariuki, author of *Mau Mau Detainee* and one of the few former detainees who has achieved some prominence in Kenya politics, first as an M.P. for Nyandarua, and more recently, as an Assistant Minister for Tourism and Wildlife.

Mr. Kariuki has for years been a turbulent and radical politician, highly critical of Government policy, and defending many points which were also raised by KPU. Even now, as an Assistant Minister, Mr. Kariuki regularly voices his disagreement with particular Government measures, although he is getting less publicity than he used to in 1969–70. This is very probably because higher placed political leaders have ordered the Voice of Kenya T.V. and radio to pay less attention to Mr. Kariuki,[104] an advice that seems to have been followed also by the Kenya newspapers.

In spite of his radical statements and of his apparently very strong desire for publicity, Mr. Kariuki has never become an exclusive Mau Mau spokesman like Bildad Kaggia up till 1969 or Mr. Kanja today. He certainly did occasionally side with the freedom fighters and the ex-detainees, as in a declaration to the Kenya Mirror at the end of 1971,[105] or in some speeches in the Kikuyu

143

Reserves, when he appealed to the Government to set up statues to Mau Mau heroes,[106] but he rarely speaks on Mau Mau in Parliament. Anyway, one has the feeling that the neglect of the freedom fighters is only one of the many injustices in contemporary Kenya he wants to have redressed.

This may have two reasons. First of all, Mr. Kariuki has never been in the forest, and it was only in detention that he became an important 'Mau Mau' leader by the uncompromising manner in which he resisted all attempts by the detention camp authorities to 'rehabilitate' him and by his restless fight for the rights of the detainees. It is therefore possible that, although sympathetic to their cause in general, he never completely identified himself with the forest fighters. It is also quite possible that he sees himself as a man with a future, and that he dreams of becoming Kenya's second, or eventually third President. If this is the case, a too close and exclusive association with the forest fighters might be a liability rather than an asset to him. In such as case, his rather general and remote concern for the freedom fighters would stand him in good stead in Kenya.

The second former detainee who achieved a position of some prominence is of course General China who, as soon as he was released from detention in June 1962, gave notice of his intention to espouse the cause of the freedom fighters. 'What am I going to do?', he answered to a question of a journalist: 'I want to go to the Government, or some of those in Legco and find out how many died. And I want advice on how to find a way for the children who have been left without mothers and fathers because of the Emergency. They have got to be given education. This is the thing I must do.'[107]

General China has not been able to realise these high ambitions, and his role in public life, as we have seen, has been very limited and discreet. It is certainly to his credit, however, that he pleaded the cause of the freedom fighters very well in his Memoirs, from which we have quoted on several occasions. Although he took extreme care to let it be known that his remarks 'should not be misconstrued as a sign of dissatisfaction with our African Government',[108] he summed up the grievances of the freedom fighters remarkably well,[109] which, for a soldier and a civil servant entirely dependent on the Government for his career, was a courageous thing to do.

144

D. Conclusions

One of the questions asked by Mr. O.W. Furley in his paper on Mau Mau Historiography presented to the 1971 Meeting of the Historical Association of Kenya was: 'How far did the political fruits and rewards after the war and struggle for independence land in the hands of Mau Mau participants?'[110] On the basis of the facts reported in this chapter, I feel inclined to say that the Mau Mau fighters did not reap so much of the fruits of independence as they had hoped for, and that the policy of the Kenya Government was found wanting in this respect.

First of all, whenever the Kenya Government did do something for the freedom fighters, this was mostly in the form of charity and 'magnanimous gestures', rather than in the form of a deliberate policy of rewarding them. The official reaction to Mr. Kanja's motion quoted at the beginning of this chapter is typical of this whole attitude. As is reported in the *Daily Nation*, 'The Government through the Minister of State in the President's Office, Mr. Mbiyu Koinange, also rejected the motion on the ground that administration officers have been instructed to take the names of genuine and needy former freedom fighters for consideration of assistance by Government. Mr. Koinange... said a lot has already been done by Government to help former freedom fighters and their relatives.'[111]

This means administrative measures in a few cases at the discretion of the civil servants who happen to be in charge of the region or the services responsible for this sort of assistance, not an official policy laid down in laws and decrees and applicable indiscriminately to all who qualify under the regulations. President Kenyatta's 'gesture' of promising training and education for 160 orphans of the Emergency on Kenyatta Day 1970, belongs to this same category of half-way measures. Picking out 160 children does not solve the problem of the orphans, which only a general law or decree could do. All these measures smack too much of charity, and yet charity is often the only assistance offered to the Emergency victims. We have already quoted the example of the Minister for Lands and Settlement who donated money to the widows of the Emergency.[112] I personally know of other examples of Ministers and leading politicians giving similar personal donations to Mau

Mau victims or who adopted orphans and paid for their education.[113]

Even if one takes into account the socio-cultural context of Kenya, where personal donations to self-help projects by politicians and other VIP's and 'charity walks' are almost daily, very well publicised occurrences, one still feels that the Kenya Government lacks and has always lacked an official policy to rehabilitate and reward the freedom fighters. This becomes all the more evident when one compares this relative failure of Kenya with what was done by Algeria for its veteran freedom fighters and their relatives. According to an official Government document, at the end of 1969, 11,000 people enjoyed a regular disability gratuity, which in the case of a 100% disablement amounted to 3,000 DA annually; 106,500 'Emergency widows' were assisted with pensions to a maximum of 1,800 DA annually and with a 20% increase for every minor child; 13,000 disabled were in the possession of special cards entitling them to free transport on public services and to other advantages, for example priority in housing, while 45,000 war-veterans were given jobs, all industrial enterprises and all commercial firms, private or nationalized, being under the obligation of recruiting at least 10% of their total labour force from amongst the ex-freedom fighters and their widows. About 10,000 veterans were employed on cooperative farms and another 2,700, living in areas where herding is the main activity, were given about a hundred sheep each. Still others had obtained licences for exploiting taxis, restaurants etc. During the first 6 years of Independence the Algerian State thus spent about 2 milliard DA on the rehabilitation of its ex-freedom fighters.[114]

Of course, these official statistics may have been somewhat inflated in order to brighten the image of the Boumedienne regime, but the important point is that one simply cannot imagine the actual Kenya Government releasing a leaflet to this effect.

I have argued, that the Kenya Government has not done enough for the freedom fighters, and that what it did might have been done in a better way. It is also sometimes said that, what was given was not given to the right people. One indeed gets the impression that it has been the policy of the Kenya Government not to reward the freedom fighters as a group, but to bestow only some favours on a few of their leaders, especially a certain number of the forest generals. According to accusations coming from ex-Mau Mau members who supported KPU, this has especially been the case with the first 400 farms that were allotted to ex-forest fighters in the settlement schemes.[115] In this way a few dozen forest leaders were 'bought' by the Government in the hope that they in turn, would help to muzzle the rank- and file of the ex-Mau Mau members and stop them from forming anti-government Mau Mau pressure groups. Of course such things are very difficult to prove, and it is quite possible that the Government critics are attributing too much scheming and too much Machiavellianism to Mr. Kenyatta's ruling team.

On the other hand, one must admit that it is easy to blame the Kenya Government, when one has no political responsibilities. After all there are also some arguments in the defence of Mr. Kenyatta and his political associates. In a way these arguments are much the same as those which prevent the Kenya Government from pushing the legend of Mau Mau too far. If, in view of the priority of nation building in Kenya, one admits the need for sponsoring the thesis that 'we all fought for Uhuru', then it becomes difficult to accept many of the Mau Mau requests which, if they were all acceded to, would lead to the creation of a sort of state-supported Kikuyu-dominated 'Uhuru-elite', a living memory of the past which President Kenyatta and many other Kenyans would prefer to forget. The same is true with regard to Mr. Kenyatta's call for *Uhuru na Kazi*. If one allows a certain number of able-bodied and healthy men to enjoy free land and all other kinds of 'free things', then the risk is great that other people, who have not been lucky enough to be admitted to this category of 'free men', might get discouraged and frustrated. Many Africans, because of the colonial past which encouraged passivity and dependence on the ruling administration, are already too easily inclined to wait for Government to bring progress and development instead of toiling for it themselves. If one gave too much privileges to the freedom fighters such tendencies would indisputably have been encouraged. This was indeed the line of argument chosen by Mr. Anyieni, the Assistant Minister for Commerce and Industry, when he spoke against Mr. Kanja's freedom fighters' motion in Parliament: 'Independence was not fought for so that people can get things without working for them. People fought for Independence so that they could have opportunities to be able to work. I think this is the President's call... If you say that you are going to treat a particular kind of people as privileged, are you not going to bring disunity to the *wananchi*?'[116]

While one may agree to a certain extent with these remarks, even then one still wonders why the Kenya Government, although right in their refusal to help able-bodied males, also gave insufficient assistance to the widows and the orphans of the Emergency, and to the maimed freedom fighters. Helping these three categories of people would have seemed the normal duty of any Government and could never have been interpreted as creating an elite or be seen as an attempt to set people apart. The same applies to the question of compensating people who, in one way or another, had lost land or other property.

Again one could argue that it must have been difficult for the Kenya Government to earmark State funds for the compensation of freedom fighters and their relatives, just as it was difficult to do this when it came to the building of monuments in honour of the Mau Mau heroes. As General China said of the situation in 1963, 'any special rewards for the Kikuyu would have looked like favouritism at that particular time'.[117]

Nothing however prevents the Government from adopting the same policy as it seems to have done recently on the issue of the building of Mau Mau monuments, that is, to allow and encourage local initiatives and eventually, to help them through the medium of local budgets. It is possible that such a policy is slowly emerging in Kenya, if the following news item is indicative of recent developments in official circles:

'The Ministry of Local Government is planning to ask county councils in all districts of Kenya to establish orphanage homes as well as homes for the aged and the physically disabled as part of the councils' social services now that the three most expensive functions – education, health and roads – have been removed from the councils' recurrent expenditure... He stressed that there are many orphans who lost their fathers during the fight for Uhuru and these must be given special consideration... Homes for such orphans, as well as all other orphans, must be established with the aid of local councils so that they may enjoy the fruits of Uhuru like other children, he said.'[118]

148

The suggestions of the Minister contain at least the germs of some kind of a solution. Just as it was possible to create a 'tribal' myth out of Mau Mau, so also it must be possible to turn the issue of assistance to the freedom fighters and their relatives at least into a regional responsibility, financed with local but official money.

Notes

Notes to 'Some Background Material: Kenya Politics, 1960–1972'

1. Soja, p. 102.
2. See Gertzel, 1970, p. 10.
3. Rothchild, p. 692.
4. *Ibid.*, p. 692. A ratio of more than 100%, as for Nairobi, is reached when virtually all children aged 7 to 13 as well as some of those below and above those ages attend school.
5. *Daily Nation*, July 30, 1970.
6. *East African Standard*, July 30, 1970.
7. Rothchild, p. 693.
8. Ruthenberg, p. 72.
9. Meisler, p. 116.
10. *Ibid.*, p. 117.
11. *Kenya Constitutional Changes*, p. 13.
12. Rothchild, p. 704.
13. *Ibid.*, p. 705.
14. Meisler, p. 119.
15. The most influent among them are probably Dr. Mungai, the Minister of Foreign Affairs, and Mr. Charles Njonjo, the Attorney-General.
16. Gertzel, 1970, p. 122.
17. Rothchild, p. 701.
18. Jones, 1965, p. 186.
19. Jones, 1966, p. 53.
20. See Fliedner, p. 22.
21. Sorrenson, p. 201.
22. *Ibid.*, p. 223.
23. See Koff.
24. *Daily Nation*, February 4, 1972.
25. Due, p. 605.

26. Koff, p. 28.
27. *Ibid.*, p .133.
28. *Daily Nation*, October 1, 1971.
29. See the *Sunday Nation*, June 22, 1969, for a revealing interview with Mr. Kariuki.
30. Odinga, p. 303.
31. Ghai, p. 373.
32. Soja, p. 102.
33. The radical viewpoints have been outlined very skilfully in Oginga Odinga's book, of which the title alone is a political programme: *Not yet Uhuru*. The moderate case has been argued in an official government document inspired by Tom Mboya and published in 1965, under the title: 'African Socialism and its Application to Planning in Kenya'.
34. See Gertzel, 1970, p. 70.
35. M. wa Kirinyaga, p. 12.
36. Kenyatta, 1968, pp. 343–344.
37. Lamb, 1969, p. 541.
38. Good, p. 129.
39. Lamb, 1969, p. 451.
40. According to then current rumours, Kaggia only took his decision after having been forced to take an oath of Kikuyu allegiance. See Lamb, 1969, p. 543.
41. Iconoclastes, p. 4.
42. Hakes, p. 154.
43. Gertzel, 1970, p. 19.
44. *Daily Nation*, November 27, 1971.
45. *Daily Nation*, June 23, 1971.
46. Ghai and McAuslan, p. 351.
47. Gertzel, 1970, p. 151. This judgement refers to the period 1966–68.
48. Wasserman, p. 12.
49. Bienen, p. 10.
50. *Daily Nation*, October 23, 1971.
51. Ghai and McAuslan, p. 309. See also, Nellis.
52. He suddenly retired from the Army a few days after the discovery of the plot, but has never been arrested. Nine less-known plotters, including one MP, were jailed.
53. See the complaints of Mr. Jack Mulwa, MP, in: Hudani.

Notes to 'The Myth of Mau Mau in Public Life and in Historiography'

1. Meister, p. 359.
2. Mitchell, pp. XVII–XVIII.
3. Brom, p. 199.
4. Carothers, p. 15.
5. *Manchester Guardian*, November 5, 1952. My italics.

6. Report to the Secretary of State, p. 4.
7. *Manchester Guardian*, December 15, 1952.
8. Brom, p. 104.
9. Perham, p. 10. It has to be said here that Mrs. Perham, as a real scholar, at least was aware that each medal has two sides, and that she rendered a great service to the African myth of Mau Mau by helping J. M. Kariuki write his pro-Mau Mau autobiography.
10. de Roock, p. 595.
11. Marris and Somerset, p. 102. My italics.
12. Furley, p. 8.
13. '*Mau Mau. What is it?*', p. 13.
14. Mitchell, p. 261. It might be suggested that this quotation throws more light on Sir Philip's subconsciousness than on the Mau Mau revolt.
15. Rawcliffe, p. 97.
16. Kariuki, p. 109.
17. *Ibid.*, p. 118.
18. Of course, J. M. Kariuki did not 'create' the African myth of Mau Mau from thin air. Some elements of it were already in existence long before he wrote his book. The term 'gallant freedom fighters', for example, which today is current terminology for the Mau Mau forest-fighters, was already used in December 1958 by Arthur Ochwada of the Kenya Federation of Labour (See Bennett and Rosberg, p. 15). The term was probably used before, but this is the oldest reference I have been able to find.
19. Rosberg Jr. and Nottingham, p. XVII.
20. Bennett and Rosberg Jr., p. 8. My italics.
21. Mr. Karari Njama preceded him in this, but his account being much more factual and objective and relatively free of 'mythology' it does not need to be mentioned in this context.
22. Itote, pp. 143–146.
23. Mazrui, 1967 A, p. 23.
24. XX, p. 1958.
25. Kenyatta, 1968, p. 189. My italics.
26. *Ibid.*, pp. 123–124.
27. See Meister, p. 181, note.
28. Kenyatta, 1968, p. 212.
29. Ali Mazrui's short but penetrating article (Mazrui, 1967 A) is the only exception in this field. Some of the paths I will explore further in this chapter were already indicated by him in 1963.
30. See, for example, *The Times*, July 22, 1963, for a drum- and trumpet declaration by Mr. arap Moi, the principal KADU-leader for the Rift Valley region.
31. Kenyatta, 1968, p. 141.
32. *Ibid.*, p. IX.
33. Mazrui, 1967 A., p. 21.
34. Kenyatta, 1968, pp. 341–342.

35. *Daily Nation*, October 16, 1971.
36. *East African Standard*, March 18, 1967.
37. *East African Standard*, May 12, 1971.
38. Jones, 1966, pp. 136–138.
39. Bennett and Rosberg Jr., p. 88.
40. Ruark, p. 7.
41. *Ibid.*, p. 225.
42. Kenyatta, 1968, p. 147.
43. Kenyatta, 1964, p. 109.
44. *Ibid.*, p. 108. P. Knauss, in his recent article 'From Devil to Father Figure' skilfully analyses the transformation of Jomo Kenyatta's image among Kenya Whites.
45. Ruthenberg, p. 68, note.
46. Bildad Kaggia. Public speech reported in the *East African Standard*, April 22, 1965.
47. *Daily Nation*, October 9, 1971.
48. *Daily Nation*, December 1, 1971. Declaration in Parliament by Mr. G.G. Kariuki, Assistant Minister for Lands and Settlement. In 1963, according to the same source, the total of expatriate owned land was 3 million hectares (or acres? R.B.).
49. O.W. Furley in the *Daily Nation*, August 26, 1971, leaves this last possibility open. Other people have also suggested to me in discussion that the destruction of Mau Mau files may have been the work of the new Kenya Administration.
50. Kenyatta, 1968, p. XV.
51. McDonald, p. X.
52. 'At the end of 1954 the Kikuyu Home Guards numbered more than 22.000,' *The Kenya Emergency*, p. 14.
53. Odinga, p. 208.
54. *Sunday Nation*, January 2, 1972.
55. *Kenya Mirror*, December 1971.
56. Ngugi wa Thiong'o, pp. 24–25.
57. Kenyatta, 1968, p. 56.
58. *Ibid.*, p. 53.
59. An interesting question is: How do the ex-freedom fighters actually see President Kenyatta? Although no definite answer can be given it can at least be claimed that one does not encounter much criticism of Mr. Kenyatta among ex-freedom fighters. 'Our President is himself a freedom fighter', seems to be the general idea, and in so far as ex-Mau Mau members are unhappy about the prevalent situation, they tend to lay the blame on the men around the President, rather than on the President himself, a quite common situation in history.
60. In August 1971, I was told by a European with longstanding Kenya experience that there is still a 100 to 200 strong group of forest fighters in hiding in the Nyambeni Hills (Meru District). My informant, whom I consider quite reliable, claims this group still existed at the end of 1969, but during my short stay in Nairobi I

have not been able to get this story confirmed either by Kenyans or by Europeans living in Kenya. Rumours also have it that there are still a few forgotten 'guerilleros' in the Nyandarua (ex-Aberdares) area. See *Sunday Nation*, May 21, 1972.

61. Amalemba, pp. 18–19.
62. *Ibid.*, p. 21.
63. Thuku, p. 100. It is interesting to note that this letter was re-published in Thuku's Autobiography that appeared in 1970.
64. See Barnett and Njama, p. 9.
65. Larson, p. 15.
66. See *Kenya Mirror*, October-November, 1971.
67. Kenyatta, 1968. p. 340.
68. See Odinga, p. 254.
69. *Daily Nation*, March 29, 1971.
70. *The Times*, February 22, 1972.
71. Unhappily I have not yet been able to obtain a copy of Prof. Ogot's paper.
72. It seems that some Loyalist's autobiographies are in fact being prepared as part of the research programme of Prof. Ogot's Department at the University of Nairobi.
73. This happened in August 1971.
74. Odinga, p. 119.
75. *Ibid.*, p. 121.
76. *Ibid.*, pp. 130–131.
77. *Kenya Mirror*, September 1971. My italics.
78. *Daily Nation*, June 26, 1971.
79. *East African Standard*, November 15, 1963.
80. *East African Standard*, December 12, 1968.
81. *Daily Nation*, November 6, 1969.
82. *Daily Nation*, September 18, 1971.
83. *Ibid.*
84. *East African Standard*, September 18, 1971.
85. *Daily Nation*, September 18, 1971.
86. Odinga, p. 132.
87. *Daily Nation*, December 21, 1971.
88. It is probable, however, that Thuku will be honoured here for his contribution to the nationalist struggle in the early twenties which was very positive indeed rather than as a Loyalist.
89. *Sunday Nation*, September 19, 1971.
90. *Daily Nation*, January 8, 1971. See also Daily Nation, May 5, 1972: 'Kimathi Plaques Go on Sale'.
91. *Daily Nation*, December 11, 1971.
92. Barnett and Njama, p. 308.
93. *Ibid.*, p. 301.
94. Wachira, 1968, p. 287.
95. *Daily Nation*, August 26, 1971.
96. *Daily Nation*, August 30, 1971.

97. See Muriithi and Wamweya.

98. Nottingham, p. 26.

99. I have used two official documents from the Ministry of Education, published in April 1968 (forms 1 and 2) and in October 1970 (forms 3 and 4). According to my information these documents were still valid at the end of 1971.

100. Loftus, p. 58.

101. Bell, p. 71.

102. *Ibid.*, p. 170.

103. *Ibid.*, p. 204. My italics.

104. Even the widely used handbook by G.S. Were and D.A. Wilson provides pupils with a rather detached and neutral image of the Mau Mau uprising in spite of the authors' contention that they 'have tried to see the more recent period from a fresh, non-colonial viewpoint' (p. V). They leave the question of whether Mau Mau contributed to the acceleration of the independence process in Kenya unanswered (pp. 274–5), and their vocabulary sometimes suggests that they have a rather negative image of the whole revolt: 'In 1946 a group of ex-army *malcontents banded together* to form the Forty Group' (p. 271. My italics); 'The Mau Mau troubles involved a large majority of the Kikuyu people but we should not forget that other communities were also *affected*' (p. 274. My italics).

105. Ogot, p. 284.

106. *Ibid.*, p. 285. According to oral information supplied by one of the editors, *Zamani* sold at least 30,000 copies in its East African edition.

107. Oral information, supplied by Nairobi publishers and booksellers.

108. Kariuki, p. 153.

109. *Ibid.*, p. 153.

110. Mr. arap Moi, *East African Standard*, February 24, 1966.

111. Dr. Mungai, *Daily Nation*, June 30, 1971.

112. Barnett and Njama, p. 489.

113. See *Sunday Nation*, January 10, 1971, and *Sunday Nation*, January 31, 1971.

114. *Sunday Nation*, January 31, 1971.

115. This may sound very strange, but only in June 1967 two forest fighters were discovered in the Mount Kenya Forest who thought that the colonialists had won the war and who claimed not to know that Kenya was independent *(Daily Nation*, June 5, 1967). It must also be noted that Mathenge like many other forest fighters was illiterate.

116. *East African Standard*, January 26, 1971.

117. See *Mau Mau Legend*.

118. He is actually Deputy Director of Kenya's National Youth Service. He was also awarded one of the highest distinctions in Kenya, the order of the Burning Spear.

119. Barnett and Njama, p. 357.

120. Itote, Chap. 26 and especially Chap. 28.
121. *Kenya Mirror*, October-November 1971.
122. 'Who was Kimathi', *Kenya Mirror*, 1968.
123. Another intriguing question crops up in this context: was it sheer accident or design that of all the Institutes of Technology that are actually mushrooming in Kenya, the Kimathi Institute was singled out for a lavish gift by the Aga Khan when he visited Kenya in the beginning of 1972?
124. See 'When Jomo was freed'.
125. It would be interesting to analyze at the end of this chapter the way Mau Mau is pictured in socialist countries and in revolutionary circles outside Kenya, but my material is utterly insufficient in this respect. I only know of a very positive article that appeared in the *Peking Review* on Kenya's Uhuru Day (see Kao Lung), and I have one incidental and rather dubious indication that the Mau Mau revolt is or was seen in Cuba as a sort of tribal, backward and 'occultist' happening, much as it was presented in the European myth (see Cooley, p. 49). It also seems that the term 'Mau-Mauing' has become part of the slang of radical Negroes and other 'Third World' groups in the US, meaning something like all aggressive behaviour short of actual physical violence, by coloured people in direct confrontation with welfare officers and other White administrators aimed at obtaining material advantages such as jobs and allowances for the 'Mau-Mauers' and their group (see Wolfe). One also hears incidentally of juvenile negro gangs or semi-political groups in the United States adopting the name of 'Mau Mau'.
126. See Buijtenhuijs, 1967 and 1971.
127. Barnett and Njama, pp. 307–308.
128. Itote, p. 189. My italics.
129. Barnett and Njama, p. 352.
130. See Buijtenhuijs, 1971, pp. 334–338 for a more detailed analysis of Mau Mau traditionalism.

Notes to 'Mau Mau in Literature and in the Popular Tradition'

1. Wachira, 1968, p. 288.
2. It is not my intention to argue that all the books on the German occupation in France and Holland are written in this epic and heroic breath. For my purpose it is sufficient that some of them are definitely in this vein.
3. Ngugi, Interview on September 18, 1971.
4. See Ngugi, 1967, pp. 120–130.
5. See, *Books 1972*, a catalogue of the East African Publishing House, Nairobi. There is, however, a play for secondary school use, which, although set in 1969, stages people whose life and thoughts mostly turn around memories of the Emergency. These people, and thus implicitly the author, do accept Mau Mau as a necessary and posi-

tive part of Kenya's history, their attitude being summed up in the following statement of one of the main characters: 'The battle was fought and won. Joy and blessing will come in ways we do not know. We shall find prosperity. We won... '(Makumi, p. 28).

6. Wachira, 1968, p. 38.
7. *Ibid.*, p. 44.
8. *Ibid.*, p. 65.
9. *Ibid.*, p. 101.
10. *Ibid.*, p. 131.
11. *Ibid.*, p. 181.
12. *Ibid.*, p. 157.
13. *Ibid.*, p. 160.
14. *Ibid.*, p. 181.
15. *Ibid.*, pp. 280–281.
16. *Ibid.*, p. 288.
17. *Ikiddeh*, p. 6.
18. Ngugi, 1964, pp. 115–116.
19. Gluckman, p. 144.
20. Ngugi, 1967, p. 28.
21. Cook, p. 18.
22. Kibera and Kahiga, p. 63.
23. *Ibid.*, pp. 61–62.
24. *Ibid.*, p. 93.
25. *Ibid.*, p. 94.
26. *Sunday Nation*, May 3, 1964.
27. Ngugi, 1964, p. 43.
28. *Ibid.*, p. 127.
29. *Ibid.*, p. 151.
30. *Ibid.*, p. 94.
31. Hower, p. 26.
32. Ravenscroft, p. 77.
33. *Ibid.*, p. 80.
34. Ngugi, 1967, p. 130.
35. *Ibid.*, p. 265.
36. *Ibid.*, pp. 223–224.
37. Hower, p. 28.
38. Ngugi, 1965 B, p. 55.
39. See, Ngugi wa Thiong'o.
40. Tejani, *Daily Nation*, May 16, 1971.
41. Cook, p. 20.
42. Ngugi, 1965 B, p. 59.
43. Ngugi, 1967, p. 280.
44. Ngunjiri, p. 43.
45. *Ibid.*, p. 44. An echo of this dialogue is to be found in J.K. Makumi's play *End of the Beginning*, where an old man and a middle aged woman are discussing the Emergency and its effects:
Old man: 'I thought you understood why your husband and your

son had to die. You know they had to die.'
Mother: 'But I am the one who suffers.' (p. 27).

46. Wamweya, p. 52, p. 53, p. 54.
47. Corfield, p. 316.
48. Kibera and Kahiga, p. 61–62.
49. *Ibid.*, p. 37.
50. Wilkinson, pp. 310–311.
51. *Ibid.*, p. 309.
52. Wamweya, p. 151.
53. *Ibid.*, p. 151.
54. *Ibid.*, p. 170. My italics. ('Wananchi' = Citizens).
55. Wachira, 1968, p. 221.
56. See Karimi. My italics.
57. Wamweya, p. 196.
58. Furley, p. 20.
59. Ruthenberg, p. 9.
60. *Ibid.*, p. 8.
61. Wachira, 1968, p. 195.
62. Ngugi, 1967, p. 120.
63. See Berque, chapter one.
64. Ngugi, 1967, p. 253.
65. *Ibid.*, p. 273.

Notes to 'The Freedom Fighters'

1. Kibera, p. 19.
2. *Kenya Mirror*, December 1971.
3. *East African Standard*, March 18, 1967.
4. *Ibid.*, June 12, 1969.
5. *Ibid.*, April 9, 1965.
6. Itote, p. 254.
7. *Ibid.*, pp. 270–271.
8. See p. 27.
9. Taylor, p. 472.
10. *Ibid.*, p. 479.
11. Ruthenberg, p. 30.
12. This Kikuyu boom probably dates from the beginning of the 1960s, gaining momentum at Independence. For the first few years following the end of the actual fighting in 1956 it would probably be more correct to speak of a 'Luo boom', many Luo having replaced the Kikuyu in urban employment, and as squatters on European farms during the Emergency. See Wood, p. 34.
13. Itote, pp. 271–272.
14. *Daily Nation*, October 23, 1970.
15. *East African Standard*, June 9, 1966.
16. *Ibid.*, January 1, 1968. My italics.
17. *Ibid.*, February 18, 1969.

18. Kenyatta, 1964, p. 104.
19. Sorrenson, p. 105.
20. *Ibid.*, p. 104.
21. *Ibid.*, pp. 105–106.
22. Odinga, pp. 125–126.
23. Huxley, p. 250.
24. *Ibid.*, pp. 250–251.
25. Sorrenson, pp. 240–241.
26. *Ibid.*, p. 181.
27. *Ibid.*, p. 181.
28. *Ibid.*, p. 211.
29. *Ibid.*, p. 219.
30. *Ibid.*, p. 3.
31. *Daily Nation*, December 12, 1971.
32. Information disclosed in Parliament by Mr. Gachago, an Assistant Minister for Lands and Settlement, *East African Standard*, November 30, 1966.
33. *East African Standard*, April 26, 1966.
34. *Daily Nation*, October 9, 1971.
35. *Ibid.*, February 2, 1972.
36. Itote, p. 260.
37. *East African Standard*, April 26, 1966.
38. *Sunday Nation*, November 21, 1971. In the Yatta area too, a few Kikuyu detainees stayed behind after the end of the Emergency (*Sunday Nation*, April 16, 1972).
39. Veen, personal information.
40. Kenyatta, 1971, p. 25.
41. Veen, 1971, p. 5, and personal information.
42. *East African Standard*, October 9, 1965.
43. *East African Standard*, October 16, 1965.
44. *Daily Nation*, May 12, 1971.
45. *East African Standard*, May 12, 1971.
46. W. Itote, p. 250.
47. *East African Standard*, July 11, 1963.
48. *Daily Nation*, September 23, 1971.
49. *East African Standard*, July 15, 1966.
50. An offer to this effect was made by a very high-placed Kenya politician but I have been unable to trace back the exact reference in the Kenya newspapers.
51. Itote, p. 250.
52. Sanger, 1964.
53. They were apparently less than 10. See Itote, p. 261.
54. *Kenya Mirror*, December 1971.
55. Kibera and Kahiga, p. 107. (Slightly adapted quotation. R.B.).
56. *Daily Nation*, March 22, 1968.
57. *Ibid.*, October 22, 1970.
58. See, for example, *Daily Nation*, December 20, 1965.

59. *East African Standard*, October 10, 1970.
60. *Daily Nation*, October 21, 1970.
61. *Ibid.*
62. Corfield, p. 316.
63. *Daily Nation*, October 21, 1970.
64. See Kariuki, p. 189, and Sorrenson, pp. 241–242.
65. Itote, pp. 259–260.
66. Sanger, 1963.
67. *East African Standard*, December 25, 1964.
68. *Ibid.*
69. *East African Standard*, January 30, 1965.
70. *Daily Nation*, February 14, 1969.
71. See, for example, *Daily Nation*, June 28, 1971; November 6, 1971; and *East African Standard*, April 29, 1972.
72. *East African Standard*, January 16, 1969.
73. *Ibid.*, May 25, 1968.
74. *Ibid.*, April 1, 1968.
75. See Auditors Reports in the NDEFFO File at the Registrars Office.
76. Private information supplied by one of the Directors of the Company.
77. *Sunday Nation*, September 5, 1971.
78. *Daily Nation*, September 6, 1971.
79. *Sunday Nation*, September 5, 1971.
80. *Daily Nation*, September 6, 1971.
81. Interviews on September 10, 1971.
82. *Daily Nation*, September 6, 1971.
83. *East African Standard*, March 29, 1968.
84. *Ibid.*, September 16, 1971.
85. *Daily Nation*, September 6, 1971.
86. To my regret I have not been able to obtain copies of these booklets.
87. Roneotyped leaflet, written in Kikuyu and found by the author on a wall in Nairobi.
88. *Daily Nation*, October 11, 1971.
89. *Ibid.*
90. *Ibid.*, November 5, 1971.
91. *Ibid.*, February 5, 1972.
92. *Ibid.*, February 5, 1972.
93. *Sunday Nation*, February 6, 1972.
94. Itote, p. 271.
95. *Daily Nation*, January 7, 1969.
96. *East African Standard*, June 24, 1964. For more details see Odinga's *Not yet Uhuru*.
97. Odinga, p. 394.
98. See *East African Standard*, April 28, 1966; May 18, 1966; and May 20, 1966.
99. *The Times*, May 2, 1966.
100. *East African Standard*, August 2, 1969.

101. The quotation is from Odinga, p. XII.
102. *Mau Mau Legend.* I have slightly adapted the quotation.
103. *Daily Nation*, May 12, 1971. My italics.
104. See Kariuki's Declaration in the *Daily Nation*, March 23, 1971. Since the summer of 1972, however, Mr. Kariuki's ban seems to have been partially lifted.
105. *Kenya Mirror*, October – November, 1971.
106. *East African Standard*, August 4, 1969.
107. See Harris, *Sunday Nation*, June 24, 1962.
108. Itote, p. 272.
109. *Ibid.*, pp. 271–272.
110. Quoted in the *Daily Nation*, August 26, 1971. (See Furley, p. 21).
111. *Daily Nation*, October 16, 1971.
112. *Ibid.*, March 22, 1968.
113. See Cox, p. 57.
114. *Algérie 65-69*, pp. 217–218.
115. *East African Standard*, May 18, 1966.
116. *Kenya Mirror*, December 1971.
117. Itote, p. 253.
118. *Daily Nation*, September 13, 1971.

Bibliography

Algérie 65/69. Alger, Ministère de l'Information, 1970.

AMALEMBA, M. A., 'Mon expérience dans l'aide à apporter à l'humanité dans le besoin', *Le Monde non-chrétien*, 53–54, janvier-juin 1960.

'Analysing Mau Mau', *Daily Nation*, August 30, 1971.

ANGAINE, J., 'Land for the Future', *Daily Nation*, December 12, 1971. (Jamhuri Supplement).

ATIENO-ODHIAMBO, E.S., 'The Modern African Library... A Running Commentary on our Times', *Sunday Nation*, March 7, 1971.

'Ban on Societies to Curb Factions', *Sunday Nation*, February 6, 1972.

BARNETT, D.L.; NJAMA, K., *Mau Mau from Within. Autobiography and Analysis of Kenya's Peasant Revolt*. New York-London, Monthly Review Press, 1966.

BELL, C.R.V., *The Road to Independence. A Certificate History of East Africa*. Arusha – Kampala – Nairobi, Longmans, 1969 (First published 1964).

BELSHAW, D.G.R., 'Agricultural Settlement Schemes on the Kenya Highlands', *The East African Geographical Review*, no. 2, April 1964.

BENNETT, G., 'Revolutionary Kenya: The Fifties, a Review', *Race*, 8 (4), April 1967.

—, 'Opposition in Kenya', in: *Opposition in the New African States*. University of London Institute of Commonwealth Studies, October 1967 – March 1968, no. 4.

—, 'The Succession in Kenya', *The World Today*, 24 (8), August 1968.

BENNETT, G.; ROSBERG, C.G., *The Kenyatta Election: Kenya 1960–61*. London etc., Oxford University Press, 1961.

BERG-SCHLOSSER, D., *The Distribution of Income and Education in Kenya: Causes and Potential Political Consequences*. München, Weltforum – Verlag, 1970.

BERQUE, J., *Dépossession du Monde*. Paris, Editions du Seuil, 1964.

BIENEN, H., 'Kenya and Uganda: When does Dissent become Sedition?', *Africa Report*, 14 (3–4), March-April 1969.

163

BLUNDELL, M., *So Rough a Wind*. London, Weidenfeld and Nicolson, 1964.

BROM, J.L., *Mau Mau*, Paris, 1956.

BUIJTENHUIJS, R., 'Un cas de tribalisme an service de la nation: le mouvement Mau Mau', *Le Mois en Afrique*, 18, juin 1967.

—, *Le Mouvement 'Mau Mau': Une révolte paysanne et anti-coloniale en Afrique noire*. La Haye – Paris, Mouton, 1971.

CAROTHERS, J.C., *The Psychology of Mau Mau*. Nairobi, Government Printer, 1954.

CHACHA, J., 'Progress Brings New Hope to Mathare Valley', *Daily Nation*, August 23, 1971.

COLLIN, C., 'Algérie, An VIII: Essai de description', *Les Temps Modernnes*, 25 (280), Novembre 1969.

COOK, D.,'A New Earth. A Study of James Ngugi's "A Grain of Wheat"', *East Africa Journal*, 6 (12), December 1969.

COOLEY, J.K., 'From Mau Mau to Missiles', *African Forum*, 2 (1), Summer 1966.

CORFIELD, F.D., *Historical Survey of the Origins and Growth of Mau Mau*. London, H.M.S.O., 1960, Cmnd 1030.

CORSARI, W., *Die van ons*. Amsterdam, De Bezige Bij, 1945.

COX, R., *Kenyatta's Country*. London, Hutchinson, 1965.

DUE, J.M., '"They Said it Couldn't Be Done". Two Agricultural Development Projects in Kenya', *Canadian Journal of African Studies*, 3 (3), Fall 1969.

DURAND, P.P., 'Customary Oathing and the Legal Process in Kenya', *Journal of African Law*, 14 (1), Spring 1970.

'Ex-Mau Mau Lead Bid to Buy Farms', *Sunday Nation*, September 5, 1971.

FAIRHALL, J., 'Plan for successor to Mr. Kenyatta', *The Guardian*, February 13, 1971.

FLIEDNER, H., *Die Bodenrechtsreform in Kenya*. Berlin etc., Springer Verlag, 1965.

FURLEY, O.W., *The Historiography of Mau Mau*. Paper presented to the Annual Conference of the Historical Association of Kenya, August 1971.

GATHERU, R.M., *Child of two Worlds. A Kikuyu's Story*. London, Routledge and Kegan, 1964.

GEORGI, U.E., 'Kanu, Kadu, Kpu: Ein Beitrag zur Typologisierung afrikanischer Oppositionsparteien am Beispiel Kenias', *Internationales Afrika Forum*, 7 (3), März 1971.

GERTZEL, C.J., 'The Role of Parliament in Kenya', *East Africa Journal*, 5 (10), October 1968.

—, *The Politics of Independent Kenya, 1963–68*. London – Nairobi, Heinemann – East African Publishing House, 1970.

GICARU, M., *Land of Sunshine. Scenes of Life in Kenya before Mau Mau*. London, Lawrence and Wishart, 1958.

GHAI, D.P., 'Contemporary Economic and Social Developments', in: B.A. Ogot and J.A. Kieran (eds.), *Zamani. A Survey of East African History*', Nairobi etc., East African Publishing House – Longmans, 1969.

GHAI, Y.P.; McAUSLAN, J.P.W.B., *Public Law and Political Change in Kenya: A Study of the Legal Framework of Government from Colonial Times to the Present*. Nairobi – London – New York, Oxford University Press, 1970.

GINGYERA – PINYCWA, A.G.G., '"Suffering Without Bitterness", by Jomo Kenyatta', *Africa Report*, November 1968.

GITHII, G., 'Press Freedom in Kenya', in: O. Stokke (ed.), *Reporting Africa*. Uppsala, The Scandinavian Institute of African Studies, 1971.
—, 'The Memories of Bitterness', *Kenya Mirror*, October – November 1971.

GLUCKMAN, M., 'The Magic of Despair', in *Order and Rebellion in Tribal Africa*, London, Cohen and West, 1963.

GOOD, K., 'Kenyatta and the Organization of KANU', *Canadian Journal of African Studies*, 2 (2), autumn 1968.

HAKES, J.E. 'Election Year Politics in Kenya', *Current History*, 58 (343), March 1970.

HARBESON, J.W., 'Land Reforms and Politics in Kenya, 1954–70', *Journal of Modern African Studies*, 9 (2), 1971.

HARLOW, V.; CHILVER, E.M. (eds.), *History of East Africa*, Vol II. Oxford, Oxford University Press, 1965.

HARRIS, M., 'I Want to Help the Orphans of the Emergency', *Sunday Nation*, June 24, 1962.

HOWARD, P., 'Le 3e Monsieur K', *Monde en Marche*, 31, novembre 1963– janvier 1964.

HOWER, E., 'The Post – Independence Literature of Kenya and Uganda', *East Africa Journal*, 7 (11), November 1970.

HUDANI, K., 'Jack Mulwa on Mkamba Politics', *Kenya Mirror*, March 1971.

HUXLEY, E., *A New Earth: An Experiment in Colonialism*. London, Chatto and Windus, 1960.

ICONOCLASTES, 'Kenya Elections', *East Africa Journal*, 6 (12), December 1969.

IKIDDEH, I., 'James Ngugi as a Novelist', *African Literature Today*, 2, January 1969.

'Is General Mirugi Still Alive?', *Drum*, 249, January 1972.

ITOTE, W., '*Mau Mau' General*, Nairobi, East African Publishing House, 1967.

JACKSON, D., 'Economic Development and Income Distribution in Eastern Africa', *Journal of Modern African Studies*, 9 (4), 1971.

JONES, N.S. Carey, 'The Decolonization of the White Highlands of Kenya', *Geographical Journal*, 131 (pt 2), June 1965.

—, *The Anatomy of Uhuru. An Essay on Kenya's Independence*. Manchester, Manchester University Press, 1966.

KAO LIANG, 'The Burning Fire of the Equator: Kenyan People's Heroic Armed Struggle', *Peking Review*, 6 (50), December 13, 1963.

KARIMI, J., 'Stranger an Emissary From "Lost" Mau Mau General', *Sunday Nation*, January 10, 1971.

KARIUKI, J., *Ode to Mzee*. Nairobi, Chemchemi Cultural Centre, 1964.

KARIUKI, J. M., '*Mau Mau*' *Detainee. The Account by a Kenya African of his Experiences in Detention Camps, 1953–60*. London, Penguin Books, 1964 (First published 1963).

Kenya Constitutional Changes. Nairobi, Kenya Research Services, 1968.

The Kenya Emergency. Report by the Kenya War Council, London, Central Office of Information, October 1954.

Kenya Leadership. Nairobi, Marco Surveys, 1967.

Kenya's Little General Election: KPU vs KANU, 1966–1967. Nairobi, Marco Surveys, 1967.

Kenyatta, J., *Harambee! The Prime Minister of Kenya's Speeches, 1963–1964*. Nairobi, Oxford University Press, 1964.

—, *Suffering Without Bitterness. The Founding of the Kenya Nation*. Nairobi, East African Publishing House, 1968.

—, *The Challenge of Uhuru: The Progress of Kenya, 1968 to 1970*. Nairobi, East African Publishing House, 1971.

KESSEL, J., *L'Armée des Ombres*. Alger – Paris, Charlot – Julliard, 1945.

KIBERA, L., *Voices in the Dark*. Nairobi, East African Publishing House, 1970.

KIBERA, L.; KAHIGA, S., *Potent Ash*. Nairobi, East African Publishing House, s.d.

KIMENA, N., 'In Kenya Now', *The African Communist*, 42, Third Quarter, 1970.

KING, K.J., 'A Biography of Harry Thuku', in K. King and A. Salim (eds.), *Kenya Historical Biographies*. Nairobi, East African Publishing House, 1971.

KIPKORIR, B.E., 'Kenya's Colonial Legacies: A Review Article', *East Africa Journal*, 8 (12), December 1971.

KIRINYAGA, MUHOI wa., *The African Communist*, 32, first quarter 1968.

KNAUSS, P., 'From Devil to Father Figure: The Transformation of Jomo Kenyatta by Kenya Whites', *The Journal of Modern African Studies*, 9 (1), May 1971.

KOFF, D., 'Note on the Kenya Election: The Contradiction of Opposition', *East Africa Journal*, 3 (5), August 1966.

LAMB, G.B., 'The Political Crisis in Kenya', *The World Today*, 25 (12), December 1969.

LARSON, C.R., 'The Search for the Past: East and Central African Writing', *Africa Today*, 15 (4), August – September, 1968.

LEGUM, C., 'The Mass Media – Institutions of the African Political System', in O. Stokke (ed.), *Reporting Africa*. Uppsala, The Scandinavian Institute of African Studies, 1971.

LEYS, C., 'Le développement de la société paysanne au Kenya', *Les Cahiers du CEDAF*, Cahier 7/1971, Série 3: Economie.

LISTOWEL, J., 'Political Strains in Kenya', *Statist*, March 26, 1965.

LOFTUS, E., *A Visual History of East Africa*, London – Ibadan, Evans, 1969.

MACDONALD, M., 'Foreword', in: J. Kenyatta, *Harambee! The Prime Minister of Kenya's Speeches, 1963–1964*. Nairobi, Oxford University Press, 1964.

MAKUMI, J.K., *End of the Beginning*. Nairobi, East African Publishing House, 1969.

MARRIS, P.; SOMERSET, A., *African Businessmen: A Study of Entrepreneurship and Development in Kenya*. London, Routledge and Kegan, 1971.

MARTIN, D., 'Kenya Waits on Jomo's Successor', *The Guardian*, August 13, 1971.

'The Mau Mau Debate', *Kenya Mirror*, December 1971.

'Mau Mau Legend', *Kenya Mirror*, 2 (14), August 1971.

'The Mau Mau Revolution as Tom Mboya Saw it', *Kenya Mirror*, October – November 1971.

Mau Mau, What is it? What lies behind it? etc. London, Church Missionary Society, 1952.

MAZRUI, A.A., *On Heroes and Uhuru – Worship, Essays on Independent Africa*. London, Longmans, Green and Co. Ltd., 1967. (A).

—, 'Mau Mau in Two Dimensions', *Africa Report*, 12 (5), May 1967 (B).

—, 'Africa's Experience in Nation-Building: Is it Relevant to Papua and New Guinea', *East Africa Journal*, 7 (11), November 1970.

MBOYA, T., *Freedom and After*, London, André Deutch, 1963.

MECK, M., 'Das Programm der KANU und seine Durchführung', *Vierteljahresberichte*, no. 38, Dezember 1969.

MEISLER, S., 'Tribal Politics Harass Kenya', *Foreign Affairs (New York)*, 49 (1), October 1970.

MEISTER, A., *L'Afrique peut-elle partir? Changement social et développement en Afrique orientale*. Paris, Ed. du Seuil, 1966.

MITCHELL, P., *African Afterthoughts*. London, Hutchinson, 1954.

MUKUNYA, B., 'Trial of Kimathi', *Kenya Mirror*, October 1968.

MULEI, C., 'KANU – A time for Radical Surgery,' *Daily Nation*, February 23, 1971.

MULESHE, R., '"The Detainee" Fred Kubai Remembers', *Kenya Mirror*, October – November 1971.

MUNRO, J.F., 'Land and Politics in Kenya: A Review Article', *Canadian Journal of African Studies*, 2 (2), autumn 1968.

MURIITHI, J.K., (With Peter Ndoria), *War in the Forest. The Autobiography of a Mau Mau leader*. Nairobi, East African Publishing House, 1971.

167

MURRAY, J., 'Succession Prospects in Kenya', *Africa Report*, 13 (8), November 1968.

'Mystery Men of the Forest', *Sunday Nation*, May 21, 1972.

'Mzee's Guiding Hand', *Daily Nation*, November 12, 1971.

NELLIS, J.R., 'Is the Kenyan Bureaucracy Developmental? Political Considerations in Development Administration,' *African Studies Review*, 14 (3), December 1971.

Ngugi, J., *Weep not, Child*. London, Heinemann, 1964.

—, *The River Between*. London, Heinemann, 1965. (A).

—, 'The Return', in: D. Cook (ed.), *Origin East Africa. A Makerere Anthology*'. London-Ibadan, Heinemann, 1965 (B).

—, *A Grain of Wheat*. London etc., Heinemann, 1967.

NGUGI WA THIONG'O, *This Time Tomorrow*. Nairobi - Dar es Salaam – Kampala, East African Literature Bureau, (1971?).

NGUNJIRI, J., 'The Return', *Zuka*, 4, December 1969.

NG'WENO, H., 'Plotters that Got Nipped', *Daily Nation*, June 14, 1971.

'"No Price is too high for Farms", say Ex-Mau Mau', *Daily Nation*, September 6, 1971.

NOTTINGHAM, J., 'The Book Trade in East Africa', *East Africa Journal*, 2 (9), February 1966.

NYAGAH, S., *The Politicalization of the Administration in East Africa: A Comparative Analysis of Kenya and Tanzania*. Lower Kabete, Kenya Institute of Administration, 1968.

ODINGA, O., *Not yet Uhuru*. London etc., Heinemann, 1967.

OGOT, B.A., 'Kenya under the British, 1895 to 1963', in: B.A. Ogot and J.A. Kieran (eds.), *Zamani. A Survey of East African History*. Nairobi etc., East African Publishing House, Longmans, 1969.

OJUKA, A., 'The Slings and Arrows of Politics', *Sunday Nation*, March 21, 1971.

OKOTH – OGENDO, H.W.O., 'Constitutional Change in Kenya since Independence', *African Affairs*, 71 (282), January 1972.

OKUMU, J., 'Charisma and Politics in Kenya: Notes and Comments on the Problems of Kenya's Party Leadership', *East Africa Journal*, 5 (2), February 1968.

—, 'The By – Election in Gem: An Assessement', *East Africa Journal*, 6 (6), June 1969.

OMINDE, S.H., *Land and Population Movements in Kenya*. London etc., Heinemann, 1968.

PERHAM, M., 'Foreword' in T. Mboya, '*The Kenya Question: An African Answer*'. London, Fabian Colonial Bureau, 1956.

PLATTER, J., 'Charles Njonjo talking to John Platter', *Sunday Nation*, November 7, 1965.

POVEY, J., 'Political Protest in the African Novel in English', in. R.I. Rotberg and A.A. Mazrui (eds.), *Protest and Power in Black Africa*. New York, Oxford University Press, 1970.

RAVENSCROFT, A., 'James Ngugi, East African Novelist', in P. Páriscy (ed.), *Studies on Modern Black African Literature*. Budapest, Center for Afro-Asian Research of the Hungarian Academy of Sciences, 1971.

RAWCLIFFE, D.H., *The Struggle for Kenya*. London, Victor Gollancz, 1954.

Report to the Secretary of State for the Colonies by the Parliamentary Delegation to Kenya. London, H.M.S.O., 1954, Cmnd 9081.

ROOCK, J.D. de, 'Achtergronden van de Mau-Mau beweging in Kenya', *Internationale Spectator*, 9 (17), September 1955.

ROSBERG, Jr., C.G.; NOTTINGHAM, J., *The Myth of 'Mau Mau': Nationalism in Kenya*. New York – London, F. A. Praeger, 1966.

ROTHCHILD, D., 'Ethnic Inequalities in Kenya', *The Journal of Modern African Studies*, 7 (4), 1969.

RUARK, R., *Uhuru*. London, Transworld Publishers Ltd, 1970 (First Published, 1962).

RUTHENBERG, H., *African Agricultural Production: Development Policy in Kenya, 1952–1965*. Berlin – Heidelberg – New York, Springer, 1966.

SANDBROOK, R., 'Patrons, Clients and Unions: The Labour Movement and Political Conflict in Kenya', *J. of Commonwealth Political Studies*, X (1), March 1972.

SANGER, C., 'Kenyatta's Kenya', *The Guardian*, December 11, 1963.

—, 'Mau Mau Leader Gets Five Years', *The Guardian*, March 13, 1964.

—, 'Kenya Retrospective', *The Guardian*, June 22, 1965.

SEMPRUM, J., *Le Grand Voyage*. Paris, Gallimard, 1963.

SINGH, M., *History of Kenya's Trade Union Movement to 1952*. Nairobi, East African Publishing House, 1969.

SOJA, E.W., *The Geography of Modernization in Kenya. A Spatial Analysis of Social, Economic and Political Change*. Syracuse, Syracuse University Press, 1968.

SORRENSON, M.P.K., *Land Reform in the Kikuyu Country. A Study in Government Policy*. Nairobi-London, Oxford University Press, 1967.

STANLEY, M., 'Heritage of Change. A Classification of Kikuyu Family Responses to Social Change and its Application to a Study of Sociological Problems of Minority Status among a sample of Kikuyu University Students', *E.A.I.S.R. Conference Papers*, June 1961, (Kampala, Makerere College, 1961).

TAYLOR, D.R.F., 'Agricultural Change in Kikuyuland', in: M.F. Thomas and G.W. Whittington (eds.), *Environment and Land Use in Africa*. London, Methuen e. Co., 1969.

TEJANI, B., 'Ngugi Forfeits Leading Place on East African Literary Scene', *Daily Nation*, May 16, 1971.

THUKU, H. *An Autobiography*, (With Assistance from Kenneth King). Nairobi etc., Oxford University Press, 1970.

VEEN, J.J., 'De Mwea Irrigation Settlement', *Landbouwkundig Tijdschrift*, 81 (1), January 1969.

—, Mwea Irrigation Settlement. Nairobi, National Irrigation Board, 1971. (Processed).

Viratelle, G., 'Le régime militaire algérien', *Revue française d'Etudes politiques africaines*, 38, février 1969.

Wachira, G., *Ordeal in the Forest*. Nairobi, East African Publishing House, 1968.

—, 'Action Needed over the Absent Farmers: Land "ceiling" is vital to stop big scramble', *Sunday Nation*, October 10, 1971.

Wamweya, J., *Freedom Fighter*. Nairobi, East African Publishing House, 1971.

Wasserman, G., 'The Research of Politics; The Politics of Research', *East Africa Journal*, 7 (11), November 1970.

Were, G.S.; Wilson, D.A., *East Africa through a Thousand Years: A History of the Years A.D. 1000 to the Present Day*. New York, Africana Publishing Corporation, 1970.

'When Jomo was freed', *Kenya Mirror*, November, 1970.

Whetham, E., 'Land Reform and Resettlement in Kenya', *East African Journal of Rural Development*, 1 (1), January 1968.

'Who was Kimathi', *Kenya Mirror*, October – November 1971.

Wilkinson, J., 'The Mau Mau movement: some general and medical aspects', *The East African Medical Journal*, 31 (7), July 1954.

Wolfe, T., *Radical Chic and Mau-Mauing the Flak Catchers*. New York, Bantam Books, 1970.

Wood, S., *Kenya: The Tensions of Progress*. London, Oxford University Press, 1962.

XX, 'La dialectique d'un mythe africain', *Revue de défense nationale*, 20, Décembre 1964.

Young, J., 'Britain Recognizes Sound Bet for Trade and Investment', *The Times*, February 22, 1972.